Freshman Guide to Writing

University of Louisiana at Lafayette

2010–2011

FOUNTAINHEAD
PRESS

Our "green" initiatives include:

Electronic Products
We deliver products in non-paper form whenever possible. This includes pdf downloadables, flash drives, & CDs.

Electronic Samples
We use Xample, a new electronic sampling system. Instructor samples are sent via a personalized web page that links to pdf downloads.

FSC Certified Printers
All of our printers are certified by the Forest Service Council which promotes environmentally and socially responsible management of the world's forests. This program allows consumer groups, individual consumers, and businesses to work together hand-in-hand to promote responsible use of the world's forests as a renewable and sustainable resource.

Recycled Paper
Most of our products are printed on a minimum of 30% post-consumer waste recycled paper.

Support of Green Causes
When we do print, we donate a portion of our revenue to green causes. Listed below are a few of the organizations that have received donations from Fountainhead Press. We welcome your feedback and suggestions for contributions, as we are always searching for worthy initiatives.

Rainforest 2 Reef
Environmental Working Group

Fountainhead Press
2140 E. Southlake Blvd., Ste L #816
Southlake, TX 76092

Web site: www.fountainheadpress.com
Email: customerservice@fountainheadpress.com

ISBN 978-1-59871-389-3
Printed in the United States of America

TABLE OF CONTENTS

Chapter One: An Introduction to First-Year Writing...1

Chapter Two: English 101...43

Chapter Three: English 102...47

Chapter Four: Forms of The Imagination: Revising Voice and Argument in College Writing...49

    Section One: Introduction to College Writing 51

    Section 2: How To Read Before You Write...58

    Section 3: Theses, Claims, and Forms of Argument 67

    Section 4: Wet Clay Language...84

    Section 5: Information Across Sentences...128

    Section 6: Using Old and New Information as a Revision Strategy...131

    Section 7: Reading For Others: Beginning Peer Review...134

    Section 8: "Just The Facts" in Introductory Paragraphs...138

    Section 9: Revision and Peer Review Go Global 141

    Section 10: Final Drafts, Final Purposes 160

    Section 11: Using MLA 168

Chapter Five: Searchers: A Quick Guide to Research and Documentation 195

    Section 1: Getting Started...195

    Section 2: Library Tools 203

    Index 208

An Introduction to First-Year Writing

❀

First-Year Writing Classes

First-Year Writing courses at the University of Louisiana at Lafayette are designed to build the skills that students will need during their university and professional careers. Because of our dedication to teaching writing skills that are applicable across the university, the English Department has created a program that begins with training in reading and writing skills in the first semester of English 101. In the second semester, English 102, these skills are developed and broadened by asking students to research and write on diverse subjects pertaining to the arts, the sciences, and many other areas of knowledge and employment that students will encounter during their writing lives.

English education itself is a unique experience. Currently, all freshmen use one of two textbooks, either *Writing Arguments* or *The Reader*, in English 101. In English 102, students use *They Say/I Say*. Additionally, your 102 course will require a second text in the form of a topic reader. But your 102 course's second textbook will vary slightly according to your instructor. Be sure to check your 102 section number when purchasing your 102 texts.

The writing instruction you receive, therefore, is unique from that of your peers in other sections of English. Yet all courses are constructed with the fundamental goal of helping you, the individual, identify and assess your abilities as a university-level writer. Thus, you will work closely with your instructor to fulfill the following list of goals by the end of 101 and 102. The First-Year Writing Committee believes that the overarching goal of your work is the ability to write a thesis-driven essay. In conjunction with this primary goal, you will

- Engage in writing as a recursive process

- Recognize the structures of argument

- Use writing and reading for learning, thinking, and communicating
- Learn to respond to the needs of various audiences

- Discuss appropriate voice, tone, and level of formality

- Integrate your ideas with those of others

The 101 and 102 process and classroom tools for achieving these goals will be discussed in greater detail in chapters two and three. Your instructor and textbooks will provide the detailed information over the course of the semester on the writing process for both individual assignments and a long-term understanding of writing that will stay with you after your first year of training and practice. The remainder of this chapter explains the prerequisites and policies of the English Department and highlights services that are offered through the university and English Department.

Prerequisites and Requirements

English 101

Students enrolled in English 101 must meet the course's prerequisites. The prerequisites are

- An ACT English score of 18 or higher (450 or higher SAT verbal)
- A "C" or better in English 90 at UL Lafayette
- A "C" or better in a developmental English class at another university
- Placement in 101 based on the UL Counseling and Testing Center's English Placement Test for students age 25 and older

If you do not meet one of these requirements, you must withdraw from this class immediately and enroll in English 90. If you fail to do so, the Director of First-Year Writing will administratively drop you from the roster, and you will not receive credit for the course.

To successfully pass English 101 and enter 102, all students must achieve a grade of "C" in their coursework and receive a grade of "C" or better on a final diagnostic essay that is issued during their final exam period. If these requirements are not met, the student will receive a grade of "D" or "F" and must repeat English 101.

English 102

Students enrolled in English 102 must also meet certain prerequisites. The prerequisites are

- An ACT English score of 28 or higher (630 or higher SAT verbal)
- A "C" or better in English 101 at UL Lafayette
- A "C" or better in an equivalent English 102 at another university
- Placement in 102 based on the UL Counseling and Testing Center's English Placement Test for students age 25 and older

If you do not meet at least one of these requirements, you must withdraw from this class immediately and enroll in English 101. If you fail to do so, the Director of First-Year Writing will administratively drop you from the roster, and you will not receive credit for the course.

In addition to these prerequisites, English 102 requires that a student receive a grade of "C" or better in their coursework and pass a final diagnostic essay with a grade of "C" as well. If these requirements are not met, the student will receive a grade of "D" or "F" and must repeat English 102.

UL Lafayette's policy states that international students whose first language is not English must take ESOL 101 and 102 to complete the writing requirement and are ineligible for English 101 and 102.

101 Prerequisite Contract

English 101   Section _____ Day _____ Time _____ Room _____

Instructor _____

Dear Student,

You are enrolled in **English 101 for the** _____ **semester.** This course has prerequisites that must be met for you to stay enrolled in this class. Please circle the prerequisite that you meet. The prerequisites are

- An ACT English score of 18 or higher (450 or higher SAT verbal)

- A "C" or better in English 90 at UL Lafayette

- A "C" or better in a developmental English class at another university

- Placement in 101 based on the UL Counseling and Testing Center's English Placement Test for students age 25 and older

If you do not meet at least one of these requirements, <u>you will be dropped from this class immediately</u> and will be asked to register for English 90. Failure to register for the appropriate English class may affect your schedule, your entrance to your major, your graduation date, and your financial aid. Students who are ineligible for 101 but remain enrolled in the class will be dropped from the roster by the Director of First-Year Writing, and they will not receive credit for the course. By university policy, international students whose first language is not English are required to take ESOL 101 and 102. International students are ineligible for ENG 101 and 102.

Your signature below indicates that you have read, understand, and meet one of the requirements for enrollment in this class.

_____

(signature)

_____

(printed name)

If you have any questions about which English class to enroll in, please go to Griffin 214 (Director of First-Year Writing Office).

Best wishes for a successful writing career at UL!

Director of First-Year Writing

101 Standard Release Form

Sample student papers often are used in universities for faculty development sessions and other purposes. You are being asked for your permission to use copies of the papers you produce throughout this semester. Your decision on whether to allow the use of your papers will not in any way affect your grade.

Teaching Portfolio

Your instructor maintains a teaching portfolio that serves as a record of the instructor's teaching and that may be used in hiring decisions (internally and with other universities), in promotion decisions, and in faculty-development situations. The portfolio includes sample student papers. Place your initials beside your response:

_____ I give permission for the use of my papers in my instructor's teaching portfolio.
_____ I give permission for the use of my papers anonymously in my instructor's teaching portfolio.
_____ Do not use any of my papers in my instructor's teaching portfolio.

Faculty-Development Sessions

The university faculty often hold sessions to discuss grading and assignment criteria, and student papers are used in these situations. Place your initials beside your response:

_____ I give permission for the use of my papers in faculty-development sessions (grading calibration exercises, discussion of assignment criteria/problems, etc.).
_____ I give permission for the use of my papers anonymously in faculty-development sessions (grading calibration exercises, discussion of assignment criteria/problems, etc.).
_____ Do not use any of my papers in any faculty-development sessions.

Future Classes

Instructors sometimes use former students' papers to illustrate writing skills/problems in current classes. Place your initials beside your response:
_____ I give permission for the use of my papers in future classes as examples of student writing.
_____ I give permission for the use of my papers anonymously in future classes as examples of student writing.
_____ Do not use any of my papers in future classes.

Student Information

First Name: _____ Last Name: _____

CLID: _____

Signature: _____ Date: _____

102 Prerequisite Contract

English 102   Section _____   Day _____   Time _____   Room _____

Instructor _____

Dear Student,

You are enrolled in **English 102** for the _____ semester. This course has prerequisites that must be met for you to stay enrolled in this class. Please circle the prerequisite that you meet. The prerequisites are

- An ACT English score of 28 or higher (630 or higher SAT verbal)
- A "C" or better in English 101 at UL Lafayette
- A "C" or better in an equivalent English 102 at another university
- Placement in 102 based on the UL Counseling and Testing Center's English Placement Test for students age 25 and older

If you do not meet at least one of these requirements, <u>you will be dropped from this class immediately</u> and will be asked to register for English 101. Failure to register for the appropriate English class may affect your schedule, your entrance to your major, your graduation date, and your financial aid. Students who are ineligible for 102 but remain enrolled in the class will be dropped from the roster by the Director of First-Year Writing, and they will not receive credit for the course. By university policy, international students whose first language is not English are required to take ESOL 101 and 102. International students are ineligible for ENG 101 and 102.

Your signature below indicates that you have read, understand, and meet one of the requirements for enrollment in this class.

_____

(signature)

_____

(printed name)

If you have any questions about which English class to enroll in, please go to Griffin 214 (Director of First-Year Writing Office).

Best wishes for a successful writing career at UL!

Director of First-Year Writing

102 Standard Release Form

Sample student papers often are used in universities for faculty development sessions and other purposes. You are being asked for your permission to use copies of the papers you produce throughout this semester. Your decision on whether to allow the use of your papers will not in any way affect your grade.

Teaching Portfolio

Your instructor maintains a teaching portfolio that serves as a record of the instructor's teaching and that may be used in hiring decisions (internally and with other universities), in promotion decisions, and in faculty-development situations. The portfolio includes sample student papers. Place your initials beside your response:

_____ I give permission for the use of my papers in my instructor's teaching portfolio.
_____ I give permission for the use of my papers anonymously in my instructor's teaching portfolio.
_____ Do not use any of my papers in my instructor's teaching portfolio.

Faculty-Development Sessions

The university faculty often hold sessions to discuss grading and assignment criteria, and student papers are used in these situations. Place your initials beside your response:

_____ I give permission for the use of my papers in faculty-development sessions (grading calibration exercises, discussion of assignment criteria/problems, etc.).
_____ I give permission for the use of my papers anonymously in faculty-development sessions (grading calibration exercises, discussion of assignment criteria/problems, etc.).
_____ Do not use any of my papers in any faculty-development sessions.

Future Classes

Instructors sometimes use former students' papers to illustrate writing skills/problems in current classes. Place your initials beside your response:

_____ I give permission for the use of my papers in future classes as examples of student writing.
_____ I give permission for the use of my papers anonymously in future classes as examples of student writing.
_____ Do not use any of my papers in future classes.

Student Information

First Name: _____ Last Name: _____

CLID: _____

Signature: _____ Date: _____

Syllabus

Your instructor will hand out a syllabus within the first week of courses. If you add late, be sure to ask your instructor for a copy. The syllabus is the blueprint for your semester. It will contain the instructor's individual policies that work in conjunction with the policies in this guide. Specific assignments and due dates will also be found in the syllabus. Your instructor's name, office number, office hours, and other contact information will be found on the syllabus as well.

Attendance

The English Department considers attendance an important aspect of writing instruction. The university guidelines allow students to miss 10% of their classes without penalty. This amounts to 4 periods for courses meeting for 50 minutes, 3 periods for courses meeting for 75 minutes, and 1 period for courses that meet once a week. Absences beyond 10% can result in a reduction to your final grade. Please note that the university does not discriminate between unexcused absences and excused absences. University policy states that the only officially excused absence is for athletic- or band-related activities. All other forms of excused absences are permitted only through the instructor's discretion. Please refer to your instructor's syllabus or speak to your instructor for details on their classroom policy. Also, students are expected to be in class the entire session. Frequent tardiness or early departure can be penalized as an absence. In extraordinary, well-documented situations, a student may schedule an appointment with the Director of First-Year Writing to discuss extenuating circumstances.

Also, registration at semester's start typically closes by the end of the first week. Your instructors will notify you of the ADD/DROP deadline. You may not add classes after this registration period closes. The university also has a final date for withdrawing from a class without receiving a grade. Placed just after midterms, this withdrawal deadline and the ADD/DROP deadline can both be found on the university's online academic calendar. Please note that all students must receive a grade of "C" or better to pass English 101 and 102 and pass their final in-class exam as well. If either of these components isn't met due to student absence, insufficient writing, or a combination of both, students must retake the course.

Mailboxes

AAll English Faculty mailboxes are located in the English Department office (Rm. 221) on the second floor of Griffin Hall (HLG). The English Department is open Monday through Thursday from 7:30 am to 4:30 pm and Friday until 12:00 pm. Student aides are on duty to provide you with assistance.

Grading Rubric

The following rubric is intended as a guide for both students and instructors, taking into account the various elements of personal and academic writing. Essays may receive an "A" grade when, in the instructor's judgment, they correspond to the "Outstanding" category as described below. At the instructor's discretion, students whose work demonstrates the strengths and weaknesses listed under "Satisfactory" may expect a grade of "B" or "C," and papers that reflect characteristics listed under "Poor" may receive a "D" or "F" grade. Keep in mind that some essay assignments may require closer attention to some skills than to others. In addition, be aware that essays are graded holistically, with the understanding that students may perform better in some areas of the rubric than in others.

	Poor	Satisfactory	Outstanding
Content	• Topic is too broad and general for a paper of its length • No clear main idea or sustained position in the paper (or argument is incredible to an academic audience) • Argument, if present, is unsupported, or evidence is insufficient • Paper is overly reliant on cliches or culturally conditioned/ ethnocentric assumptions and bias • Sources, if used, are used inappropriately (data dump, awkward integration, unintentional plagiarism, etc.)	• Topic is manageable for a paper of its length • Position/argument is comprehensible even if not clearly stated • Amount of evidence is sufficient • Demonstrates critical thinking (ability to recognize complexity, biases, and stereotypical representations; distinguishing fact from opinion) • Use of sources is appropriate; no serious problems with integration of other materials	• Topic is narrow enough to allow for a rigorous, nuanced treatment of the subject • Thesis is stated clearly • Evidence is ample to support position taken • Contains some acknowledgment of opposing/divergent views • Sources are used purposefully and strategically, integrated seamlessly
Organization	• Introduction does not orient the reader to the concerns of the paper or contextualize the subject of the paper • Arrangement of the paper is haphazard and random • Paragraphs do not have transitions that guide the reader from one idea to the next • Conclusion is absent or abrupt	• Introduction is recognizable even if it is not always reader-based • Paragraphs generally treat one idea at a time • Attempts at transitions between paragraphs are made, even if they are awkward • Conclusion provides some closure to the argument, even if only a summary of the main points	• Paper contains a clear, reader-based introduction, development, conclusion • Logical, smooth transitions between sections • Plan of development stated (forecasting statement, self-announcing structure to argument) • Conclusion does more than just summarize the paper; restates the thesis in a fresh way or includes a gesture (call for action, unresolved questions, etc.)
Language Issues	• Frequency of error (of any type) seriously detracts from the content of the paper	• Grammar, punctuation, and spelling are mostly correct • Student shows command of language (word choice/ vocabulary) • Varied sentence structure	• Paper is virtually free of error • Writer shows an unusual felicity with regard to word choice, turns of phrase (ex. uses obscure words, bon mots) • Sentence structure is complex but not cumbersome

Plagiarism Statement

The *Undergraduate Bulletin* sets forth the University's philosophy on plagiarism and academic dishonesty as follows:

> An essential rule in every class of the University is that all work for which a student will receive a grade or credit be entirely his or her own or be properly documented to indicate sources. When a student does not follow this rule, s/he is dishonest and s/he defeats the purpose of the course and undermines the goals of the University. Cheating in any form therefore can not be tolerated; and the responsibility rests with the student to know the acceptable methods and techniques for proper documentation of sources and to avoid cheating and/or plagiarism in all work submitted for credit, whether prepared in or out of class. (400)

The following pages further describe plagiarism particularly within writing courses, offering general guidelines and examples for using sources in essays.

Plagiarism Defined

Plagiarism is claiming someone else's work as your own. Ideas circulate freely in an intellectual community, and intellectual inquiry often depends on use of ideas borrowed from others. Responsible writers, however, indicate their debts to others by clearly citing borrowed material. Plagiarism occurs when writers fail to cite their borrowings. Auto-plagiarism consists of plagiarizing yourself. In the context of your coursework as a student, auto-plagiarism would occur if you resubmitted any of your own work—whether a complete assignment or only part of it—as if it were freshly submitted.

Plagiarized work is easy to recognize because it does not clearly indicate borrowing. It is full of facts, observations, and ideas the writer could not have developed on his or her own and is written in a style different from that of the writer. By clearly indicating your debts to other writers, you can both avoid plagiarism and call attention to your own original ideas.

Integrating Sources

Understanding the different ways you can incorporate source material into your writing is crucial to avoiding plagiarism:

Quotation ("quote" for short): a word-for-word copy of someone else's words. Indicate a quoted passage by enclosing it in quotation marks ("") or, if it is longer than four lines, by setting it apart from the main text in an indented block. The source of the quotation must also be cited, either in the text or in a footnote or endnote.

Paraphrase: a restatement in your own words of something your source has said. One purpose of paraphrasing, as opposed to quoting, is to put something into words your audience will understand. For example, articles in popular science magazines often paraphrase more difficult articles in science journals. Putting something into your own words is an important intellectual activity in its own right: it shows that you understand and can work with the material. Putting an idea in your own words does not make it yours. Although neither quotation marks nor block indention are needed, a paraphrase must be cited.

Summary: resembles a paraphrase but is much shorter and follows the sources less closely than a paraphrase does. You must cite the source that you are summarizing.

Citation: identifies the source of a quotation, paraphrase or summary. Citation practices vary considerably in different types of writing, but most academic and professional writing requires a full citation in the text, in a combination of brief parenthetical citations in the text and complete bibliographic entries in a list of Works Cited, or in footnotes or endnotes.

Types of Plagiarism

1. **Direct Plagiarism:** This is copying a source word for word without indicating that it is a quotation and crediting the author.

2. **Borrowing work from other students:** There is nothing wrong with students helping each other or sharing information, but you must write your own essays. This includes having another student dictate to you as you write their words down. Turning in a paper that someone else has written is an especially severe case of direct plagiarism.

3. **Vague or Incorrect Citation:** A writer should clearly indicate where borrowing begins and ends because not to do so, though it seems innocent, is plagiarism. *This is why it is so important to learn a citation style such as MLA style* (see MLA Style section for more information). Sometimes, a writer cites a source once, and the reader assumes that the previous sentence or paragraph has been paraphrased, when most of the essay is a paraphrase of this one source. The writer has failed to indicate his borrowings clearly. Paraphrases and summaries should be indicated as such by surrounding them with citation-—at the beginning with the author's name, at the end with a parenthetical

reference. The writer must always clearly indicate when a paraphrase, summary, or quotation begins, ends, or is interrupted.

4. **Auto-plagiarism:** This happens when an author plagiarizes his or her own writing. Students' best work usually occurs through revisions of previous drafts. But auto-plagiarism takes place when a student presents any prior writing, usually from another course or school, as entirely fresh work for course credit. A previous assignment—whether in whole or part—may **not** be offered as if it were a fresh submission to a course instructor.

5. **Mosaic Plagiarism:** This is the most common type of plagiarism. The writer does not copy the source directly, but changes a few words in each sentence or slightly reworks a paragraph, without giving credit to the original author. Those sentences or paragraphs are not quotations, but they are so close to quotation that they should be quoted directly or, if they have been changed enough to qualify as a paraphrase, the source should be cited.

Penalties for Plagiarism

No plagiarized paper will be accepted for credit in any Writing Program course at the University of Louisiana at Lafayette. This includes partially plagiarized papers. As a student, you assume responsibility for any plagiarism that occurs in your essays.

Please note that the possible penalties for plagiarism, as set forth in the *Undergraduate Bulletin*, are severe: "The University considers both cheating and plagiarism serious offenses. The minimum penalty for a student guilty of either dishonest act is a grade of "zero" for the assignment in question. The maximum penalty is dismissal from the University" (400). If your instructor suspects that you have plagiarized in a paper, s/he will fill out an Academic Dishonesty Report. The instructor will then forward this report to the Dean of Students, where it will be kept on file. In addition to the penalty you can expect from your instructor, the Dean may, depending on the severity of the offense, impose any number of additional penalties. These penalties may include but are not limited to the student being fined, required to take an ethics class, placed on probation, or expelled from school. Any student suspected of plagiarism will have the opportunity to discuss the matter with the Dean of Students or the Director of First-Year Writing and will, following the proper procedures, be given the opportunity to appeal any decisions or penalties.

Why Students Plagiarize

Some students are tempted to paraphrase because they find writing college-level essays difficult or intimidating. Such students sometimes become frustrated when an essay on which they have worked long and hard is returned with many corrections and a low grade. Frustrated and afraid of failure, they may resort to copying an essay word for word or making only a few slight changes in the wording.

Rather than plagiarizing, these students should seek assistance from their instructor, from the Writing Center, from a special tutor, or from the Counseling Center, which can provide assistance in dealing not only with a learning disability, but also with frustration, fear, and stress. The Writing Program offers intensive tutorial courses in writing. For information, see the

"Writing Center" section in this guide or call the Writing Center directly (482-5224).

Other students write well enough but find plagiarism tempting because they fear earning a grade lower than they or their parents expect, have fallen behind in their coursework and feel that they lack the time to write a competent essay, or feel that they cannot handle the assigned task or generate good ideas on the subject.

Start writing, even if the writing begins as a summary of some other piece of writing, and you will usually discover that you have something to say. If you fall behind, talk with your instructor. He or she may penalize you for submitting work late, but late work is preferable to plagiarized work. If you feel overwhelmed by your course work and unable to keep up, arrange to visit a counselor at the Counseling Center. He or she can help you learn to manage your time and the stress of university life better.

Plagiarizing an essay is never an acceptable solution.

A Case of Plagiarism

Richard Marius, in his statement on plagiarism for Harvard University, cites a case of mosaic plagiarism. G. R. V. Barratt, in the introduction to *The Decembrist Memoirs*, plagiarized from several works, including *The Decembrists* by Marc Raeff. In one passage, Raeff had written:

> December 14, 1825, was the day set for taking the oath of allegiance to the new Emperor, Nicholas I. Only a few days earlier, on November 27, when news of the death of Alexander I had reached the capital, an oath of allegiance had been taken to Nicholas's older brother, Grand Duke Constantine, Viceroy of Poland. But in accordance with the act of renunciation he had made in 1819, Constantine had refused the crown. The virtual interregnum stirred society and produced uneasiness among the troops, and the government was apprehensive of disorders and disturbances. Police agents reported the existence of secret societies and rumors of a coup to be staged by regiments of the Guards. The new Emperor was anxious to have the oath taken as quickly and quietly as possible. The members of the central government institutions—Council of State, Senate, Ministries—took the oath without incident, early in the morning. In most regiments of the garrison the oath was also taken peaceably.

Barratt presented the same paragraph with only a few words and details changed:

> December 14, 1825, was the day on which the Guards' regiments in Petersburg were to swear solemn allegiance to Nicholas I, the new Emperor. Less than three weeks before, when news of the death of Alexander I had reached the capital from Taganrog on the sea of Azov, an oath, no less solemn and binding, had been taken to Nicholas's elder brother, the Grand Duke Constantine, viceroy of Poland. Constantine, however, had declined to be emperor, in accordance with two separate acts of renunciation made in 1819 and, secretly, in 1822. The effective interregnum caused uneasiness both in society and in the army. The government feared undefined disorders—with some reason, since police agents reported the existence of various clandestine groups and rumours of a coup to be effected by guardsmen. Nicholas was anxious that the oath be sworn to him promptly and quietly. At first it would seem that he would have his way; senators, ministers, and members of the Council of State took the oath by 9 A. M. In most regiments of the garrison the oath was also taken peaceably.

To see why this is mosaic plagiarism, compare these two versions line by line. What changes has Barratt made? Why do you think he made these changes? Why is this a case of plagiarism even though Barratt has made changes?

Guidelines for Proper Use of Sources

1. Enclose direct quotations in quotation marks. If the quotation is longer than four lines, indent it in block format. In both cases, cite the source by using MLA in-text parenthetical style and by entering the source in the Works Cited page.

2. Use in-text parenthetical citation to cite paraphrases or summaries. Any key phrases that you borrow word-for-word should go in quotation marks.

3. Cite opinions, interpretations, and results of original research.

4. In general, do not cite statements of widely accepted fact; but when following a source closely, cite it even if the material is widely accepted fact. If you are unsure if something is a "widely accepted fact," then you should probably cite it. See your instructor if you have any questions about facts.

Ways To Avoid Plagiarism

1. When in doubt, CITE! It can never hurt to over-cite or cite when you don't need to.

2. Give yourself plenty of time to research and write your essay, so that you do not feel pressured because a topic proves unworkable at the last minute. When writing a paper that uses sources, give yourself time to digest the research and synthesize your findings.

3. Take careful research notes that include full bibliographic citations. If you forget to write down the bibliographic data, you may be tempted not to bother with the citation.

4. Make it a habit to put parenthetical citations for all the sources you borrow from in each draft you write.

5. Keep a good documentation guide handy (i.e. your handbook) when you are doing your research and writing your paper.

6. Have confidence in yourself. Even the best writers are often unaware of their good ideas and think they have nothing to say when their writing says a lot. Original ideas come from working closely with the ideas of others, not from flashes of inspiration.

7. Know where to get help. Start with your instructor and ask questions about citations about which you are not sure. Besides your instructor, you can consult a tutor in the Writing Center for help with your writing. The reference librarians at Edith Dupree Library can help you with your research. The counselors at the Counseling Center can help you with problems like time management, stress, and learning disabilities. Their services are confidential and free of charge. Finally, your academic advisor can help you put your course work in perspective.

Conclusion

Learning how to use sources is one of the most important things you will learn in college. By using sources well and by clearly indicating your debts to these sources, your writing gains authority, clarity, and precision. Writers who plagiarize lose the advantages of belonging to an intellectual discourse community. If plagiarizers are professionals, they may be barred from practicing their profession, or their work may not be taken seriously. If they are students, they will carry the stigma of having plagiarized. Instructors will be suspicious of their work and will be unwilling to support any of their future efforts, write recommendations for them, or even work with them at all. Plagiarism is one of the worst mistakes anyone can make. The best way to avoid it is to be scrupulous about indicating quotation, paraphrase, and summary.

101 Plagiarism Contract

I have read and understand the University of Louisiana at Lafayette's plagiarism information statement. I know that intentional plagiarism is a punishable offense with penalties ranging from a zero on the assignment to expulsion from the university. I also know that unintended plagiarism can occur through improper citation and/or borrowing but is still punishable. To avoid unintentional plagiarism, I will consult with my instructor when I have questions.

Student's Name: (Print) _____

Course: _____ Section: _____ Instructor: _____

Semester and Year: _____

Student's Signature: _____ _____

Date: _____ _____

102 Plagiarism Contract

I have read and understand the University of Louisiana at Lafayette's plagiarism information statement. I know that intentional plagiarism is a punishable offense with penalties ranging from a zero on the assignment to expulsion from the university. I also know that unintended plagiarism can occur through improper citation and/or borrowing but is still punishable. To avoid unintentional plagiarism, I will consult with my instructor when I have questions.

Student's Name: (Print) _____

Course: _____ Section: _____ Instructor: _____

Semester and Year: _____

Student's Signature: _____

Date: _____

UL Library

Edith Garland Dupré Library is centrally situated on the main campus of the University of Louisiana at Lafayette at 302 E. St. Mary Blvd. The library is open to students, faculty, staff, and the public. In 2000 two major construction projects were completed: (1) the renovation of the building which had existed since the middle of the 1970s and (2) an addition to the back of that building which resulted in double the amount of previous floor space. The Instructional Materials Center (IMC), a branch library, serves students and faculty from the University by providing materials to be used in classroom instruction on the elementary and secondary levels. It is located in Maxim Doucet Hall, Room 101. Dupré Library contains almost 1 million bound volumes and 2 million microform units. Some 4000 serial titles are currently under subscription and backfiles are being collected in print and non-print format. Special collections include: U.S. government documents, Louisiana government documents, materials pertaining to the history and culture of Acadiana (in the Jefferson Caffery Louisiana Room), the University Archives and Acadiana Manuscripts Collection, the Folklore/Oral History Collection (contains a unique repository of tape-recorded Acadian folk tales, songs and oral histories) and the Louisiana Colonial Records Collection (consists of microfilm copies of original documents related to the development of Louisiana from 1605 to 1805). Funds from a BORSF grant received in 2003 are being used to establish a collection of commercial recordings of Cajun, Creole, zydeco and swamp pop music. Most of the library's collections are available online through the *iLink* catalog. Patrons may access *iLink* over the Internet from home, office, or campus. Educational materials housed in the Instructional Materials Center may be searched separately or in conjunction with a search of Dupré Library's holdings.

For more information, please visit the library link on the University of Louisiana at Lafayette's homepage.

General Library Assignment

Name: _____ Course/Section No.: _____

Part I: Library Online Catalog/ iLink

Access the iLink catalog on any of the terminals designated for iLink use in the library; for more detailed instruction on searching iLink refer to the blue handout "Welcome to iLink" or download from the Bibliographic Instruction web pages at: http://library.louisiana.edu/Bib/instruct.shtml.

1. What is the call number to the book titled *A Lesson Before Dying* by Ernest Gaines? _____

2. List any other book written by Ernest Gaines. _____
   _____
   _____

3. List the title to a book **about** Ernest Gaines works. _____
   _____
   _____

   [Tip: For books ABOUT an author (or anyone), type the name in by last name, first using the Words or Phrase search mode]

4. Which floor of the library are the PS call numbers located?

   _____

5. List any title of a video recording of an Ernest Gaines book. [Tip: Do an iLink Advanced Search and type "Ernest Gaines" in at the "Words or Phrase" search field, then scroll down to "Format" and select "MARC Visual Material" and then hit the Search button.]

6. What is the call number to the journal titled *The Explicator?*
   [Tip: Search within the "Periodical Title" mode for journal titles]

7. Does the library subscribe to the journal titled College Literature?

Part II: Database Exercise

8. List a multi-disciplinary database that covers all subjects.

9. Using the *Databases by Subject* index, list any 2 databases specific to Literature.

10. Perform a search in *Academic Search Premier* on any topic and print a full-text article.

Peer Reviews

In addition to writing your own essays, in English 101 and English 102 you will also read, analyze, and critique the ideas of others. You will read essays written by professionals, as models for your own writing and as sources for ideas. You will also be asked to read and evaluate the essays of other students in the class as part of the revision process. These peer review sessions are vital as a learning experience for you, the reviewer, as well as giving the writer essential feedback before she/he revises. Consequently, it is of paramount importance that you attend class each day. Your instructor will announce a specific attendance policy during the first week of classes; please pay attention to this policy and take it seriously.

General Peer Review

Author: _____   Reviewer: _____

1. Can you identify the purpose of this essay through a specific claim? If not, why not? Does the amount of specificity in the introductory paragraph adequately prepare the reader for the rest of the essay?

2. What is the writer's tone and attitude toward the subject matter? Toward the audience? Is the tone too serious, too sarcastic, or too caustic? How does this reflect on the writer's attitude toward the subject matter and the writer's sincerity?

3. In conjunction with number two, which particular details or sections of the essay are convincing? Which are unconvincing?

4. Can you follow the essay's order clearly? If not, where does the writer's presentation of the material become disordered? What minor points or topics appear out of order?

5. Is there any absent information that would make the piece more convincing or understandable? Are there details or information that do not seem necessary to the writer's purpose for writing?

6. Do the paragraphs contain topic sentences and signals that clearly announce the direction and intention of essay? If a paragraph is confusing or difficult to follow, what is confusing? The language? The thought? The order of the thoughts?

7. Does the style of the piece include a mix of short and long sentences to create a readable rhythm and pace? Would some sentences be clearer if separated into shorter sentences or rewritten? Does the writer use the passive voice when unnecessary?

8. Is the language appropriate to the writer's subject? Is the prose free of heavy vocabulary, clichés, or worn-out phrases that deny the writer and reader more exact and clear presentation of idea? Has the writer followed proper grammar, punctuation, and MLA format and citation? If rules have been broken or changed, did it seem justified?

9. Does the writer have a closing that wraps up all of the major and minor thoughts that were previously unfinished?

Peer Review – Persuasive Essay

Author: _____ Reviewer: _____

1. What is the thesis statement? Is it strong, specific, and direct?

2. Comment on the "lead" or introduction. Does it effectively pull you in, make you interested in the essay and the topic being discussed? What about it specifically does or does not successfully accomplish this?

3. In general, what do you consider the target audience of this essay? Is it clear that, generally speaking, the author is directing his or her arguments towards any particular group or person? Is it an appropriate target audience for this essay? Along these lines, what suggestions do you have regarding target audience?

4. What are the main arguments presented by the author to support his/her thesis? Note whether or not each argument is convincing. Note how you might improve any weak arguments. Do the arguments tie back into the thesis, or are faulty connections made between the thesis and its support?

5. Does the author make effective use of emotional language without going overboard? If yes, what areas are particularly effective? If no, where might the writer "sharpen up" the language?

6. Is the opposition acknowledged? Are opposing arguments successfully rebutted?

7. How strong is the essay's conclusion? Does it leave a lasting impression while also summarizing the main arguments of the essay? How might it be improved? Be specific.

8. Comment on the essay as a whole. Is it effectively persuasive? Is it well-written? Is the structure organized and easy to follow? What can the author do to improve it between now and the next draft?

Peer Review – Research Paper

Author: _____   Reviewer: _____

1. What is the thesis statement? Is it strong, and does it lead you into the rest of the paper? Does the rest of the paper tie directly back into the thesis?

2. Comment on the introduction. Does it effectively pull you in, make you interested in the essay and the topic being discussed? What about it specifically does or does not successfully accomplish this?

3. Does the author use signal phrases in appropriate areas in order to introduce the sources he/she is using in the paper? If not, where might be a few appropriate places to do so?

4. Find all direct quotes. Can you tell where they begin? Does s/he use quotation marks? Does the author cite his/her sources in the text correctly, using the author's name and page numbers? Make any corrections or suggestions you can.

5. Find all cases in which the author uses summaries/paraphrases. Can you tell where they begin? Are citations handled correctly? Make any corrections or suggestions you can.

6. Does the author have enough supporting evidence and secondary source material, and is that material organized in a logical manner? Which areas still need more and/or better support?

7. Comment on the organization of the paper. What type of strategy does the author use to structure and organize his/her discussion of the evidence? Is it effective? How might it be strengthened?

MLA Citation

English Departments use the MLA (Modern Language Association) conventions when presenting and documenting essays and research. In all your English courses, you should use the MLA documentation style unless instructed otherwise. Courses in other departments often use other citation styles. For a full explanation of MLA documentation and format, you can consult Chapter Four of this book or the appropriate sections of your course textbook.

The Writing Center
Griffin Hall, Room 107
Call 482-5224 for the most current hours of operation.

Philosophy

The University Writing Center is a free service, staffed by experienced graduate and undergraduate peer consultants and writers. Our staff prides itself on creating a comfortable and productive environment for writers of all skill levels, in all disciplines, at any stage of the writing process. Located on Griffin Hall's first floor, the Writing Center provides a service far more valuable than proofreading and editing. Peer consultants focus on helping writers improve their arguments, organize their ideas, and design strategies for a consistent and reliable writing process. Our approach is student centered and individual, structured around the belief that writers improve by involving themselves in their subjects and collaborating with other writers through every phase of the process. Furthermore, the Writing Center peer consultants are students themselves, conscious of your scholastic experiences and willing to respond with suggestions that take into account your schedule and lifestyle. Services include:

1. Brainstorming for topic ideas
2. Outlining and Organizational Strategies
3. Assignment interpretation
4. Revision plans
5. Research plans
6. Citation conventions

Although walk-ins are accepted, we highly recommend making appointments in advance. An open-access computer lab is located next door for document printing and Internet access. We also house a writing reference library with the latest style manuals, dictionaries, and composition textbooks.

Preparing for your Writing Center Appointment

Because the Writing Center is devoted to instilling long-term strategies that can help you beyond each individual assignment, our advice is in the interest in making you a better writer through discipline, practice, and an enthusiastic attitude toward your writing project. As a result, we recommend scheduling appointments far in advance of your project's deadline. In addition, please consider bringing:

1. Assignment Descriptions

2. Assignment rubrics

3. Class notes

4. Assigned Reading

5. Typed drafts

Because our primary concern is improving your writing practices, the Writing Center provides a far more valuable service if you visit early and often, long before the assignment is due.

Policies and Procedures

1. Each writer is entitled to two fifty-minute sessions per week.

2. Students who are more than ten minutes late for an appointment must reschedule.

3. Content of appointments is confidential. The Writing Center does not divulge any student information to instructors without student consent.

4. The Writing Center is managed by students and committed to improving students' university experience and performance. Our goal is to address the writer's development, not adhere to the instructor's grading policies. As result, while projects that have been workshopped in the Writing Center show significant improvement, we cannot guarantee higher grades.

Writers of all levels who consistently visit the Writing Center have reported repeated success and satisfaction with their work. Please stop by and consider utilizing the writing center throughout your career here at the University of Louisiana at Lafayette.

OWLs

OWL is the acronym for "Online Writing Lab." These online labs support the work of writing centers across the nation by providing information on grammar, punctuation, and sentence style, as well as plagiarism and various citation styles. Whether you have visited the Writing Center or not, you will find the basic answers to your particular questions about sentence-level writing skills. Students who spend time on the skills addressed by OWLs often see their grades improve because of clearer sentence structure and fewer sentence-level errors. The most acclaimed OWL can be found at http://owl.purdue.english.edu, but a simple internet search will turn up many useful labs.

About Moodle

Moodle is a widely used Learning Management System, installed here at UL Lafayette as an alternative to Blackboard. Courses created under Moodle can be configured as desired by the instructor, to provide a syllabus, contact information, a calendar, course lectures (in various formats), assignments, assessments (quizzes, surveys, choices), discussions (via forums) and virtual classrooms (chatrooms). Students and instructors can communicate with all classmates/ groupmates via the class or group forum, and can email individuals shown in the Participants listing. A student can choose to receive email from all forum postings, or to visit the forum interactively and see which postings are unread. Students may upload files for assignments that require responses, and see comments their instructor may provide along with an assignment grade. An instructor may create a wiki in which their class participates as collaborators on a common work. Also, a glossary can be provided by an instructor to allow terms within online text to be highlighted and their definition or corollary information to be retrieved via a mouse-click.

To access **Moodle**, simply click on the Moodle button on the **ULink** portal, or browse directly to http://suze.ucs.louisiana.edu:8080/moodle/ and login using your UCS username (CLID) and password. Your home page will show any courses you take (or teach) under "My Courses." Click on the desired course and you will see the available course content in the middle of the page, with various options shown to the left and right of the page. In particular, a "Recent Activity" block will show, for example, recent additions to course content.

The Southwestern Review

The *Southwestern Review* is the University of Louisiana at Lafayette's in-house literary journal edited by graduate and undergraduate students in Creative Writing. It features poetry, short fiction, non-fiction, and drama by faculty, graduate students, and undergraduates, and it is illustrated with student art work. Submissions are accepted during most of the fall semester. Check the billboards of Griffin Hall or the Creative Writing Department's link on the English Department website for details.

Ann Dobie Outstanding Freshman Essay Awards

Each spring the English Department sponsors the Ann Dobie Outstanding Freshman Essay Awards, open to all full-time freshmen. The awards are split into two categories, one for Outstanding Narrative/Personal Essay and one for Outstanding Research Paper. Your 90, 101, 102, or 115 instructor will announce this year's deadline at some point during the spring semester. Students are allowed and encouraged to revise their essays before submitting them for award consideration. Please check with your instructor or with the Director of First-Year Writing, Room 214 HLG, for the official guidelines to the 2009-10 Outstanding Freshman Essay Awards.

Contestant's Name: _____

Title of Essay: _____

Instructor's Name: _____

Course Number: (Circle One) 90 101 102 115 Course Section: _____

Semester: (Circle One)   Spring   Fall

Contestant's Contact Information:

Email: _____

Phone Number: _____

Address: _____

_____

_____

Chapter Two

English 101

❊

Course Description

As mentioned at the beginning of Chapter One, English 101 is the first half of the Freshman English sequence that introduces students to college writing. With its full title of **English 101: Introduction to Academic Writing**, the focus of 101 is to introduce students to the critical thinking, reading, and writing skills required in the university and beyond. The course will focus on writing effective and well-argued essays. The final paper for 101 includes some research as an introduction to the research-oriented semester of 102. During the 101 semester, each student will write 15-20 pages of polished, formal prose while also completing readings and informal assignments.

English 101 Outcomes & Goals

The purpose of English 101 is to introduce students to the critical thinking, reading, and writing skills required of them in the academy by focusing on rhetorical awareness and argument. All assignments for English 101 should be designed with the following outcomes and goals in mind:

In the course of writing thesis-driven essays, students will:
- Engage in writing as a recursive process
- Recognize the structures of argument
- Use writing and reading for learning, thinking, and communicating
- Respond to the needs of various audiences
- Discuss appropriate voice, tone, and level of formality
- Integrate their ideas with those of others

Formal Assignments

1. Evaluation and Summaries: Evaluating sources and writing summaries are valuable tools for reading comprehension, for developing a sense of structure, and for assessing the value of source material. Opportunities to practice the skills of evaluating and summarizing will be given through the readings.

2. Formal Essays: You will write both working and final drafts of approximately four or five fully developed personal, informative, and/or persuasive essays (each from 800 – 1500 words).

3. Timed Writings: You will be given the opportunity to practice writing in preparation for exam-taking in other courses and for future writing under pressure.

Informal Assignments

In addition to the above formal writing activities, you will also be required to complete informal writing assignments. While these assignments may not always receive grades by themselves, credit will be given for satisfactory completion and this credit will affect the final grade for the course. These assignments may take the form of journal writing, responses to readings, in-class invention work, class notes, and freewriting exercises. The purpose of these exercises will be to provide you with an opportunity to practice your writing without being formally evaluated.

Audience

Writers do not write just to reveal personal feelings or just to inform or just to persuade; they write to reveal feelings or inform or persuade someone about something. If you are writing to explain and/or change human behavior, you can accomplish this only if you are addressing a specific audience. Consequently, instructors of 101 may provide such questions as the following to help you analyze your audiences early in the composing process:

1. What does the audience already know about the subject?

2. What do I think that my audience needs to know about my subject? What do I want my audience to know?

3. Of what value will awareness of my subject be to my audience?

4. How will my audience react to my subject? What steps must I take to ensure that my audience will read and appreciate what I have to say?

By the end of this course, you should be accustomed to beginning a composition with a concept of what particular audience or audiences you wish to reach.

Invention

Invention, or as it is now more frequently called in English classrooms, "prewriting," is a stage many novice writers do not know about and, therefore, miss in their composing processes. Consequently, English 101 places much emphasis in this area. The invention process involves exploring a subject to discover its many possible topics and developing fluency on organizational patterns for an essay. You will be given many strategies to help you in the invention process, including brainstorming, freewriting, sharing, discussing, clustering (also known as mapping), looping and cubing. They may not all work for you, but you should try each one until you find a method that works for you.

An important goal of 101 students is to begin to develop ideas in depth. In order to achieve this goal, your instructor will introduce some basic research techniques as a way of finding evidence to support your ideas. You may also be asked to provide in-text references and proper citations of your research.

Collaborative Work

Many 101 instructors employ group work as a tool of instruction. Research has shown that groups tend to outperform individuals in areas such as creativity and development. Today, groups are essential to many corporations and businesses, as well as on campuses and in classrooms.

Group effectiveness is a product of the interaction of individuals with a common goal. In 101 classes, students may discuss readings and develop ideas about the writing processes, intent and language usage of authors. Groups will learn to critique one another's essays with the intention of helping your group members improve their writing skills and learning techniques to improve your own essays.

Multiple Roles of the Collaborative Reader

There are many roles people perform in groups. Some of these relate to helping the group perform its tasks, while others relate to maintaining the group and relationships among members. These roles are ways in which any person (either a member or a designated leader) can help a group work on any task. When any of these functions are omitted, the effectiveness of the group declines:

Initiator/Contributor: Helping the group get started; proposing goals; suggesting new ideas, new definitions of the problems, new attack on problem or organization of what has already been discussed.

Information Giver: Offering facts or additional useful information; relating one's own experience to group problem to illustrate a point.

Opinion Giver: Stating an opinion or belief concerning a suggestion or one of several suggestions; expressing what one thinks or feels; focusing on values rather than offering further facts.

Information Seeker: Asking for clarification of suggestions that have been made; requesting additional information or facts that will help.

Chapter Three

English 102

❧

Course Description

English 102 combines the writing and thinking practiced in English 101 with the research process. Officially titled **English 102: Writing and Culture**, this course explores cultural themes and intensifies the research process. You will build on and advance thinking, reading, and writing skills learned in 101 while focusing on rhetoric and research. In addition to your rhetorical textbook, each section of 102 typically requires a second text, a course "reader" that will supplement your writing and research. Be sure to purchase the correct reader for your section of 102. Each formal paper for 102 will include research of some form. During the semester, students will write 20-25 pages of polished, formal prose while also completing readings and informal assignments.

English 102 Outcomes and Goals

The purpose of English 102 is to build on the writing skills students learned in English 101 by focusing on academic research. Each section of 102 is based around a cultural theme. All assignments for English 102 should be designed with the following outcomes and goals in mind:

In the course of writing thesis-driven research essays students will:
- Engage in writing as a recursive process
- Develop essays around a specific purpose
- Explore the nature of academic discourse and examine what "counts" as evidence in academic writing
- Integrate outside sources into their own writing
- Apply the appropriate conventions of citation style and mechanics

Instructors may add to these goals and outcomes.

English 102 Diversity and International Requirement

Students should be aware that English 102 has been designed to fulfill the required goals of stressing diversity and international awareness as set forth in the Undergraduate Bulletin. The university recognizes English 102 as meeting these requirements and serving an important role in the intellectual development of students.

Plagiarism Reminder

As you start your semester of intensive research and citation, remember that plagiarism can be both intentional and unintentional. Please refer to Chapter One's **plagiarism** section to refresh your awareness of borrowed material.

Chapter Four

Forms of The Imagination: Revising Voice and Argument in College Writing

❊

Introduction

Playing with language is something that we all do every day. Typically, we play with language while joking around with friends in informal settings. Often, we only play with language while speaking because speaking is informal, or we only play with print language in informal settings like email, Myspace, and Facebook—settings where no one is watching or grading. Yet the same principles that allow us to withhold ideas, speed up ideas, or speak indirectly or by implication are the same principles that reshape any communication in any setting.

This book has two purposes: to comfortably introduce you to college writing and to show you how to play with the language of formal writing. If there is a single word to capture the purpose of this book, it is *revision*. If there is a single word to capture the advice of this book, it is *awareness*. An awareness of how to play with language will demystify the revision process.

This book does not have detailed information on how to start writing a paper; that is not this book's purpose. However, you will find that Chapter Nine contains examples and discussion of how students have used personal experience to begin their research and writing, and Chapters Two and Seven discuss how your personal knowledge and a writing assignment meet to create an essay. Personal experience is always a great way to begin investigating a subject. In general, starting an essay, known as *prewriting*, will be discussed by your instructor and elsewhere in your required texts.

This book mimics the process of writing and revising college writing assignments. You'll start with advice on reading strategies, move on to rough ideas in need of sentence and paragraph revision, then close the book with examples of polished final drafts. Thus, unlike other textbooks, you'll find that many of the examples in this book are not examples of "perfect" writing. Often, a person learns by fixing a broken something, not by talking about a new, unbroken something. Tinkering is more educational than memorizing an instruction manual, and playing in the mud is more fun than reading about playing in the mud.

Some former students have been kind enough to contribute their writing, much of it raw and unpolished, so that you have a textbook full of good ideas that are not yet complete. Each of the rough drafts in this book contains the seeds of a polished essay, but the essays often lack a consistent way of seeing or organizing all of the information that the writer includes; by reading the included comments and suggestions, you'll get an idea of how other students' strategies for writing an essay succeeded and faltered. Chapters Six, Seven, and Nine contain essays of this type, and the road blocks in these essays are those that instructors often see in student writing. There is a good chance these problems will be your own at some point. Reading these chapters may help you diagnose problems with your own writing, and they will also give you a glimpse inside the mind of the college instructors who give you advice and grade your essays. For polished, finished essays, see Chapter Ten.

The past and present editors of the Guide would like to thank Benjamin Ng, Brooke St. Julien, Kimberly Hillhouse, Skyla Wilson, Brandon Plaisance, Anthony White, Raul Viera, Lyle Miller, Amy Guilbeau, Patrick Fitzpatrick, and Morganna Ochoa for contributing their writing to this book. Because they have generously offered essays that show their writing at various stages, the process of writing has been reproduced, allowing us to see and talk about what writing really look like start to finish. In addition, the current editor wishes to acknowledge the invaluable contributions of Liberty Kohn, former editor and UL-Lafayette Ph.D. In particular, Chapter Four is entirely Liberty's creation.

SECTION ONE

Introduction to College Writing

❊

Getting Started

What is College Writing?

The classroom looks the same. Squeaky clean chalkboards. Fresh textbooks with unbroken seals. Knapsacks not yet carrying scars from heavy loads and wet weather. Students wide-eyed in either confidence or bewilderment....

Yet college writing is not the same as high school writing. You may have blown like a breeze toward straight As in high school English courses, or you may have heavily trudged toward other grades. However, as a college student you are not destined to repeat your past successes or failures with various aspects of the English language. College writing will offer you the chance to redress the "type" of English student you are. If your clear, concise, poetic language drew accolades from your teachers in the past, it may still. If knowing every grammar rule backward and forward produced neverending high marks in the past, your grammar knowledge will be incredibly useful.

Yet college writing is not the same as high school writing. The skills and tasks will focus on writing and research to prepare you for *critical thought* and *rhetorical awareness* for your future collegiate and professional careers. College writing will need to be mechanically sound. Spelling, punctuation, grammar, readable sentences, and well-managed paragraphs: For these skills you can thank each of your previous English teachers, as well as yourself. Each of these "mechanical" skills will be the basis for your foray into your development as a communicator. You will add an awareness of how each writing task changes the criteria through which you construct your ideas.

College writing instructors will focus on issues that you may not have fully explored during past English courses. During your years in college English classes, you will discuss some eternal notions that the most ancient of writing theorists realized surround all writing and communication. By the time you leave your first-year writing classes ideas such as audience and purpose, exposition and argument, critical thought, and having a "process" will be just a few of the ideas and vocabulary that you take with you.

If your memories of high school English are writing an essay on the tragic qualities of Hamlet, or learning about The Great Depression while reading *Grapes of Wrath*, you'll certainly have opportunities to discuss these topics in college English, but reading Shakespeare and Steinbeck won't be the focus of your writing class. Discovering different ways to analyze and interpret Shakespeare and Steinbeck may be. More importantly, you'll be asked to focus on critical thinking as a process applicable to any text, whether a newspaper article, a fairy tale, a novel, a satirical cartoon, or a political ad on late-night television. Specific courses will focus on specific writing tasks and types of texts so you won't be asked to do high school English better. You'll be asked to do something different: college writing.

Argument and Critical Thought

Argument proper seeks to persuade or convince your audience to accept a claim as truthful or reasonable. Potentially, your argument may hold a higher goal of getting your audience to act upon that truth claim. Argument is not a synonym for "fight," nor should it lead to holding a grudge. Although war metaphors abound when it comes to describing argument, argument as defined in college and intellectual realms has more to do with "debate" and, hopefully, cooperation. You may find yourself and others raising your voice or voicing your frustration, but in proper argument you are doing so through means of expressing your views of both a problem and a solution.

Not everyone will agree with your claims. Most arguments, unlike boxing matches, do not have a clear winner. The purpose of argument is to share at two or more viewpoints and solutions for a given subject. Along the way, each participant is expected to include only relevant information and claims that present both a valid and lucid background and framework for the problem, as well as for the implementation of the solution. Because the goal of argument is not winning, but understanding, it has been suggested that the best metaphor for argument is not war, but "conversation." The metaphor of a conversation aptly sums up the goal of all intellectual argument. You have entered a room where many people are talking. They've been talking a long time. You enter and listen for awhile. You begin to understand much that has been argued and decided before you entered, and you hear what everyone is saying now. After listening, you speak, saying what seems sensible to you, then you leave as others enter and begin to listen. This view of argument depends upon cooperation, as well as "listening" to the research and opinions available to you.

Argument is a system analyzed by many ancient civilizations. In the Western tradition, the Greeks were the first to discuss and outline the ethics and the structures of argument. The ethics of their argumentative system centered around the same premise as modern argument in the United States: democracy. Not all arguments deal directly with government, of course, but the Greeks knew what we still believe today. If all people belong to the decision-making body of society, then each member of society must be educated and must have the ethics of greater society guiding their purposes and goals. These goals will vary from person to person depending upon their experience, learning, and beliefs. Each individual's unique background gives them strong feelings on a subject. You may not be able to change their beliefs despite using the structures of argument expertly, and they may not be able to change your beliefs either. People's past is a primary factor of what they find acceptable, and this has long been known to argument theorists and to anyone with a healthy dose of common sense. Each person has their own view to share with the world. You may not convince someone wholly that your opinion is the correct one, so the goal of argument is always to listen openly to new viewpoints and to open someone else's mind to your viewpoint.

Although there are many systems of argument when one examines theoretical nuts and bolts, there are some basic ideas common to all. You will see these basics of argument not only in your college English courses, but in all of your courses, from philosophy to physics. Later chapters will explore these methods in greater detail, giving you a system to evaluate your own argument or someone else's argument and to generate a variety of argumentative thoughts.

One of the most basic (and possibly oversimplified) argumentative structures is the following:

Claim/Opinion:
Reason/Grounds:
Counterargument/Opponent's Opinion:

Examine the following exchange for claim, reason, and counterargument:

> **Bill**: Listen little sis, I need the car on Saturday night because I promised the guys I'd drive them to the movie.

> **Tiffany**: Listen big brother, you had the car last Saturday because you were driving your friends to the movies.

> **Bill**: Even though it was your weekend to have the car, you didn't even go out last Saturday night. I only was able to use it because it was sitting in the garage.

You can see the claims and reasons, as well as ongoing reasons and counterarguments, from Bill and Tiffany. Each makes a claim in their opening statement followed by a "because" statement that gives their reason for their belief. This is not to say that all "reasons" in argument are signaled with a "because" statement or that all reasons can be summed up in a single sentence. However, you can see how even the most everyday argument works from a claim and reason basis. You can also see how the claim and reason format would continue for the siblings as they continue to try to persuade each other that each has a right to the car on Saturday night. Perhaps most important, you can see differing sets of values behind each siblings claim to the car. While Bill trusts in a concrete every-other-week rotation, Tiffany believes that her forfeiture and Bill's use of the car during her forfeited week entitles her to the car, breaking the every-other-week rotation. Thus, each has a different "ethic" for how a car should be shared, and each argues on claims and reasons specific to their ethic.

Yet it is also easy to see where we get the idea of argument being heated by passion and possibly resentment. Each side takes a turn. A huge gap exists between what each desires. Sometimes one side must "lose" what they desired. However, in civics as well as many careers, you'll be expected to "civilly" argue a point and persuade your audience without looking like you'll hold a grudge or throw a tantrum should a decision not work in your favor. You'll also be expected in professional and civic situations to abide by the basic argumentation structure. If you don't, your audience, also attuned to the structures of argument, will most likely sense your breakage of the rules and not trust you. We'll examine a variety of frameworks for strong and weak argument in future chapters.

Do people break argumentative structures and ethics? Of course. Although the reasons can vary with the situation, it may often be because their argument has no strong claims or reasons, yet the person does not wish to change their views or goals. This may not be the only reason, as in the following:

"Mommy, why is the sky blue?"
"Because why?"
"Just because...."

When a child asks this question, they may receive the "just because" answer because their parent does not feel like explaining the answer—for example, if mommy is an astrophysicist who knows exactly why the sky is blue, but knows that her audience, a toddler, will not understand the science of the blue sky. As budding intellectuals though, you'll be expected to both explain your argument energetically and to critically question any argument you come across. "Just because" answers are not seen as acceptable to those who are trained in the rules of ethical and knowledgeable argument.

If the "just because" answer comes from someone familiar with the structures of argument, it can often derive from a person who knows they have a weak argument but does not care, or the "just because" answer can derive from a writer or speaker who does not have the topic knowledge to make a stronger argument. The first reason is not forgivable by the rules of ethical argument; however, the second means the person simply has not done their research. This is not a crime, and not having an answer to every question is not a crime either. A lack of topic knowledge simply means that you need to do more research to discover and understand both the problems and potential solutions before claiming to present a fully informed argument. Socrates was the first to develop and question both the ethics and structure of argument. His advice is still sound today: "The unexamined life is not worth living."

Part of college's mission is to teach examination of the world around you. This is why it is impossible to passively absorb and remain unchanged by all the material and experience of your college years. By the time you leave college, you'll be so used to examining claims and evidence for strengths and weaknesses that you won't be aware that you are doing it. Reading critically will simply be a part of your reading process. Thinking critically will be a part of your everyday thought, just as you may not have been unaware that you were engaging in the timeless strategy of claim and reason every time you bargained with a sibling. We'll return to argument in Chapter Three of this book.

Reading in College

What is reading? Ask someone this question and the answer they are likely to give will be along the lines of "looking at the words." Perhaps a stronger answer may be akin to "figuring out what the essay means." Most of us read passively at most times of the day. And why shouldn't we read passively? We aren't the experts, right? Whoever wrote and delivered the messages we receive, from political statement to junk mail, must certainly be playing fair and must certainly know about their subject, right....

Reading includes recognizing words that are strings of letters, and reading includes trying to get the point of the text. But if you are reading to write or reading to analyze, you must read to believe and to doubt—both are active reading processes. Most of the day, we read by the rules of a shallow passive version of belief. That is, we don't question in-depth the messages that are communicated to us. We accept them and go on with our day. This may be because most messages aren't highly argumentative, and they do not have major bearing on our life.

The successful college reader will begin by reading for an understanding of the author's thesis. Yet as this reader reads, they are also examining if the author is playing by the rules of fair argument and asking if the claims, reasons, and truths are sensible and based on solid knowledge of the topic's background. This is a strong version of the believing game. Yet, even if a reader finds that the author's argument seems solid and probable, they are still formulating an equally valid counterargument based upon their own beliefs. Thus, one reads to "believe"—to see if the author has created an informed and sensible argument that potentially solves the problem; yet the educated reader also reads any argument with their own values and thoughts on the subject, using the text in front of them to explore issues and claims they may not have previously encountered or answered fully. An attentive, active reader is always producing potential counterarguments and wondering what opinions and evidence exist other than those the text in front of them presents.

A variety of opinions exist on nearly all, if not all, issues in our society. One example of how a reader may read actively to understand *and* critique can be found in the debate over video game violence and its effect on young users. If an essay argues that child violence has increased since the release of violent video games in the last several decades, one can believe, but one can also start asking questions of this thesis. An active critique would question whether the violence could be influenced by other societal factors, such as less parental supervision or poverty. An active critique may also question whether there is evidence that disagrees with a thesis linking video games and violence, such as any research existing on rates of violence for children with violent video games and children with no exposure to violent video games.

Strategies for being an active reader will be presented in an upcoming chapter, but for now you can become a better reader by simply doing two things: Reading with a pencil in your hand and taking notes on both the author's ideas and your own feelings on and critiques of the author's claims. We'll return to the topic of effective reading in Chapter Two of this book.

Knowledge, Research, and Your Field

Returning to argument as "conversation," college instructors understand that the courses they teach (and that you are taking) require knowledge you do not necessarily have but are building. The knowledge is often encyclopedic and found in books. From time to time, your personal knowledge may be highly useful. Do not discredit it. Your own experience can be a useful tool to begin to formulate opinions, especially on issues that are based upon opinion and are highly arguable. You will know the basics of many social issues, as well as the typical claims and counterarguments, because of the massive amount of media exposure prominent social issues receive. Yet after you begin to formulate an opinion and research that opinion, you will often find yourself moving briefly into a more "encyclopedic" world of facts, histories, and expert opinions that are on a much more subtle level of thought than you'll typically see on television or hear in soundbytes. In college and in life after, class readings, library books, and internet searches will expediently introduce you to the basic conversation of a subject so that you can create a sensible opinion quickly. After researching through these opinions, your final argument will often be a mix of your older values informed and perhaps changed by your more subtle research and understanding.

Most subjects you will study in college will fall into the category of encyclopedic knowledge— subjects such as nineteenth-century American political history, small animal zoology, subatomic structures, or the crisis in Darfur all require book learning. So college requires hitting the books and owning knowledge, not just waving at facts and arguments as you pass by. So *how* you read becomes important not only for daily success on your homework: How you read determines how much you understand. Critical readers that both believe and doubt tend to "own" the opinions and ideas of a reading quicker. So a reader's strategy may determine how much usable information one will retain and whether or not the reader can factor this new information into the "big picture" when writing.

Ultimately, the point of choosing a major in college is to take as many courses as possible that relate to a certain field to give you the "biggest" big picture. Your reading strategy in college will determine how big the frame of your picture is, how well you can write as both a "believer" and a "doubter," and how well you can speak as a trustworthy authority on a given subject. Your professors, your future employers, and the community at large will be all ears every time you attempt to give them the big picture through a feasible argument filled with researched knowledge.

Not all subjects are argumentative. Science is famous for it's ability to experiment and produce universal physical truths that cannot be disproven with humankind's current knowledge. So scientific truths and the field of science are viewed as the least argumentative. Reading in the sciences may often require readings for memorization of procedure and outcome for whatever knowledge you are studying. The social sciences and the humanities, however, are famous for argument. Both the outcomes (particular findings through application of a method) and the methods (a particular way of analyzing an object or subject) of both the social sciences and the humanities are open to critique through sound argument. If you are in any of the fields comprising the social sciences or humanities, you should always have an understanding of why you chose your methodology for your particular topic, and you should be prepared to defend it as a proper methodology to explore your subject and make argumentative claims about your subject's qualities.

Genre and Your Field

I mentioned earlier encyclopedic knowledge, the knowledge of one's discipline or field through books and coursework. I also mentioned that experience is important as well. This is why good grades *and* an internship will make you a well-rounded addition to your field, a better candidate for the job you want, and a benefit to a society that depends on your field's success. Yet a different type of knowledge works in conjunction with this field knowledge. This knowledge is *communication knowledge*. This is the valuable knowledge that English and Communication courses will be teaching you, even if you are not an English major and do not consider yourself an "English" person.

Basics exist in all forms of communication. For example, audience, purpose, argumentative frameworks, and other principles which are field specific are found in a different variety in every field. After all, we must communicate our knowledge, and we find it easiest to talk to each other in consistent forms so that our messages are as clear as possible. Each different form is often referred to as a "genre," which is simply a term for a "type" of communication form. Each of the following is a genre specific to a purpose or task. Writers use them to deliver their message to us in a predictable and persuasive form that we understand because of our previous experience with the forms.

Science Lab Reports
Business Memos
Recipes
Rent Checks
Sales Flyers
Case Folders
Book Reviews
Medical Reports

Naturally, some genres are broad and break down into smaller genres. Medical reports, for instance, come in a wealth of varieties.

These forms play a crucial role in delivering our message in an understandable way. They are roadmaps guiding us toward predictable destinations, even if we do not know what we will find when we get there (some type of solution or hypothesis, most likely). If you defy a genre's conventions, you risk losing your audience or sending indirect messages that you don't intend. The indirect messages may interrupt your audience's understanding of your argument. They may try to understand why you've chosen a non-traditional format to present your information and lose focus on your ideas; or the indirect messages may tell your audience that you haven't yet mastered the communicational competence of your field. Each is potentially devastating to the information you wish to get across to your audience and the argument you wish them to consider.

Much of the introductory college writing course is dedicated to developing an awareness of genre and communication formats. English teachers, after all, do not have encyclopedic knowledge of everything about which their students write. English instructors, as well as all instructors in other departments, do have a great facility to analyze an argument and see the big picture even in areas where they do not have expertise. This questioning process is one skill they will pass on to you. The second skill they will pass on to you is the specialty of English departments—an awareness of language and its ideas, better known as genre and argument.

When one gets down to the subject of genre, there are too many genres in each of dozens of fields. English courses cannot cover all genres. Even the classes in your major may not cover all genres. You will learn many of them only when life demands it. Thus, English courses prepare you to begin to evaluate how information, whether cold scientific facts or blood-boiling argument, is structured in typical situations. Your instructor will most likely discuss how the essay forms you are assigned can be models for your own similar writing purposes. You can use this rhetorical knowledge for your own field in the future. Because argument has a prominent place in democracy as well as in many collegiate and professional fields, your English instructors will spend much of their time on the various methods of sound argument. Exposition, or explaining, will be equally important: Exposition is also an important type of communication; often, it buttresses argument. Once you are adept with genres, exposition, and sound argument, you can deliver your opinion, secure that the knowledge of your field as well as your opinion are understandable to your audience.

SECTION 2

How To Read Before You Write

❖

Effective Reading Strategies

As mentioned in the opening chapter, reading strategies come in many different forms. A good reading strategy will always be constructed upon the goals for reading. Reading for a college course is obviously different than reading a murder mystery. The latter is read for fun. The former is read for information. Yet beyond reading for information, there is always a higher purpose. You must ask yourself the following:

What is the point of the article and/or author?

Why am I reading this? (your purpose separate from the writer's purpose or point)

While the first question is an old one, the second question will help guide your thoughts as you read. Here are some potential answers to the second question:

1. You may be reading to introduce yourself to a subject you will discuss in class.

2. You may be reading to learn more about a subject already introduced in class.

3. You may be reading to learn about a sub-field related to previous class readings.

4. You may be reading an article that complicates a theory or opinion you have already read in class.

5. You may be reading material already covered in class in an attempt to "own" the knowledge.

There are many more reasons to read inside of each of these oversimplified categories. The type of things that you concentrate on and write in your notes should reflect your knowledge of the subject. If you are not familiar with the subject, you must remember the basic framework of the subject. This may be the "story" of how a scientific theory or mathematical equation works, start to finish. Or it may be the "story" of how merchant's diaries across several centuries can tell us about changes in American history or the American mindset. Or it may be the "story" of how a society's music holds in it the values of that society itself. But if the subject is not familiar, you are reading so that you can repeat, in your own words, the basic outline (start to finish) of the explanation or argument you have read.

If you are reading on a subject already familiar to you, then you may be reading "against" the text or reading to "doubt." That is, you may be reading to find holes in the argument. While this may be tough in some subjects (the sciences), more philosophical classes will thrive on you reading "against" an opinion. You will be expected to create counterarguments or find arguable evidence as you go. Or you may be reading to better master the intricacies of material you already know. College courses are designed this way in general. You learn the basics, then you learn sub-areas to fill in your growing knowledge. While a list of "things to do" when reading cannot radically change how you are used to reading, good readers are made, not born, and no one but yourself can remind you *why* you are reading.

You will often times encounter new information and different types of argument and organization, and your purpose for reading may not always be clear. When this happens, you may read an entire night, yet not really remember much of what you read. Your verbal summary may take no more than several seconds, and you'll wonder how an hour's reading resulted in such a small summary. Part of the reason for this is the human brain. It cannot remember everything. However, focusing on a framework—the "story" or sequence your reading presents—will help. Repeating as much of the story or sequence as you can, mid-reading, will help lock up the new information in your memory. Good notetaking aids this process. Repeating the story or sequence as if it is yours will undo the experience of feeling blank after an hour's worth of reading. You will have begun to own the knowledge, and it will feel like your knowledge, not the essay author's knowledge.

Not all instructors may be exemplary in telling you why you are reading and how this new knowledge combines with older knowledge. Some instructors prefer, to some extent, to keep you unprejudiced in your reading. This can be helpful because your instructors are not leading you toward certain conclusions. You can always ask what will be important in a reading ahead of time. However, taking control of your reading strategy is your best bet. One basic mode of reading is comparing and contrasting. Why? Because our brains take in all new knowledge by assimilating it with old relevant knowledge. Before reading, you wish to jot down notes or simply take a moment and think about what you know about the subject of the assigned reading. If there is nothing on your mind when you begin reading, there most likely won't be as much on your mind when you finish reading.

Knowing how to find the framework, story, or sequence may not require reading straight through an article or essay. You can sometimes use your communicational knowledge to move around and get the gist of a reading before you read it closely. If you do this, you may be approximating reading something twice because you are understanding the basics before you begin reading closely.

Choosing Criteria for Reading Strategies

Although there are many strategies, each of them dependent upon your purposes and goals, having a process will help. In addition to answering the *why am I reading* question, ask yourself:

A. What do I know about this subject?

B. What type of piece is this (genre, structure, prose style)? Based on the field it comes from, how will the information most likely appear? How can I use this to my advantage?

C. How will I remember and categorize new information?

Answering these questions may lead you to the most helpful strategy. Some reading strategies are listed below. In addition to asking yourself if the following are efficient ways of reading, ask yourself if there are potential problems in each reading strategy.

1. Read essay straight through, no rereading

2. Read essay without a pencil

3. Read introduction and conclusion first

4. Read only for topic sentences

5. Read for topic sentences first (scanning). Reread thoroughly after you have working knowledge of the subject of the article or essay.

I would suggest that Number Two is a bad idea. Number One is most likely impossible. We all loop back to reread, and this is good for the memory and understanding. Note taking is an essential aid to your memory, and as you know, your memory is all too human. If you sometimes forget where your car keys are, why would your memory remember all the stories and sequences of college learning unless you actively ask it to do so? Repeating these stories and taking notes are your best bets to retaining information for later use. Looking ahead to main ideas, rather than backward, can help you understand the logic or sequence of an essay's content whenever you are feeling lost or wondering what the point is. Unlike murder mysteries, reading the last page first does not spoil the reading. Instead, you may have a better idea what you are reading for in the first place.

Texts: Patterns, Structures, and Signposts

Certain terminology surrounds writing. Become familiar with this terminology. It will help you discuss your own writing, your peers' writing, and classroom reading assignments. Different essays will have different forms of these terms, but the patterns, structures, and signposts of writing will always be there. The goal is to make these terms yours. For that, you'll need to be able to describe them to yourself and others in your own language. You may wish to discuss as a class what the working definitions and limits of these writing features:

Thesis
Topic sentence
Subordination
Main idea
Secondary idea
Support/evidence
Expert opinion
Facts/data
Testimony
Transition
Direct statement
Indirect statement
Audience
Purpose
Personal knowledge
Research knowledge

Genre Excerpts With Exercises:

Let's look at the following texts and text excerpts. I have selected each text because it is unique from the others; yet each essay contains all or some from the above list or writing features. Also, to challenge you, many of these essays are missing the bulk of their information. Why? Because I want you to decide on an effective reading strategy before you simply "dive in" and start reading. Each essay contains features that can stop a reader cold in their tracks if that reader is looking for immediate understanding or to "just start reading." After scanning or reading each text or excerpt, stop and think for a moment about the challenges it provides to a reader who reads for information and argument.

So try two things as you read: First, try out various reading strategies from section C above; second, apply the terms from "Patterns, Structures, and Signposts" to specific sections of the essay. This second idea will create discussion of genre, which is highly important when choosing an appropriate reading strategy.

Essay #1:

The following essay is an anthropological essay.

Opening of Essay #1:

Parental Selection: A Third Selection Process in the Evolution of Human Hairlessness and Skin Color

Judith Rich Harris

"I don't want to kill her. This little girl is too beautiful. See how lovely and fair her skin is?" (1)

Those words were spoken shortly after childbirth by an African woman named Chuko, a member of the hunter-gatherer people known as the !Kung. The story was told to an anthropologist by Chuko's daughter, Nisa. Chuko had planned to kill the newborn – by burying it before it took its first breath – because her previous child, Nisa's younger brother Kumsa, was too young to be weaned. Rearing the new baby would thus jeopardize Kumsa's chances of survival. But when Chuko saw the new baby she had a change of heart. The baby was allowed to live and she did indeed grow into a beautiful girl.

Marjorie Shostak, the anthropologist who recorded Nisa's story, explained that infanticide (now against the law) was until recently the only reliable method available to !Kung women for spacing their babies. The !Kung were not unusual in their use of this draconian method of birth control. According to the evolutionary psychologist Steven Pinker, "Infanticide has been practiced in all the world's cultures" (2). In former times deciding whether to keep the newborn was often the first decision a mother had to make after she gave birth. But the decision was never made lightly, and a particularly appealing newborn had at least a slim hope of changing its mother's mind. The ethologist Irenäus Eibl-Eibesfeldt described another such incident: an Eipo woman who had decided in advance to abandon the baby if it should be a girl but changed her mind after her daughter was born (3). [...]

Closing of Essay #1:

My hypothesis about the evolution of pale skin is a good deal more difficult to test. No one doubts that this change must have occurred after members of our species occupied Europe and Asia; as far as I know, no one doubts that it occurred after our species developed language and culture. Thus, my hypothesis does not differ from prevailing views in regard to timing. Soft-tissue evidence from frozen ice men will be of no use.

Evidence will therefore have to be sought in a roundabout way. For example, I asserted that light skin provided no survival benefits to the ancestors of modern-day Europeans. If it is found that modern light-skinned humans have longer or healthier lives than their darker-skinned neighbors, at least at some latitudes, that would be evidence against my hypothesis. Another prediction is that females should, on average, have lighter skin than males. There already appears to be enough evidence that light-skinned females win higher-quality mates – males with higher status – than their darker-skinned sisters.

Alas, the beautiful fair-skinned baby whom Nisa's mother decided to rear, rather than kill, cannot provide us with any evidence, pro or con. Kxamshe, as she was called, died in her early teens, apparently of malaria.

Instructor and Student Questions for Essay #1:

1. From only this article's opening, can you predict the argument of this article?

2. Would you consider the opening paragraph a "straight-ahead" and direct statement on the evolution of pale skin?

3. Would you consider the closing paragraph a "straight-ahead" and direct statement on the evolution of pale skin?

4. To what extent are these complications dependent on the author's choice in presenting information on a single case study about a mother and child? If there were statistics on pale skin evolution, rather than a single mother and child, would the introduction be more understandable?

5. If someone were lost during this or a similarly arranged essay, what reading strategy would you suggest they use?

Essay #2:

EMPLOYMENT PREFERENCES AND SALARY EXPECTATIONS OF STUDENTS IN SCIENCE AND ENGINEERING
By Dorceta Taylor

The number of students pursuing degrees in science and engineering (S&E) has grown over the last two decades. During that time, our ability to track changes and predict enrollment trends has improved. Consequently, there are reliable data on the number of students enrolling in and graduating from S&E and other higher education programs. There is also a robust body of data and publications on employment trends and workforce characteristics in S&E fields (CAWMSET 2000, NSF 2000, NSB 2006). Nonetheless, there are scant data on the employment preferences and salary expectations of S&E students (NSF 2001). As a result, we know little about what kinds of workplaces current S&E students are willing to work in and what kinds of salaries they expect to earn when they enter the workforce. This article focuses on the employment preferences and salary expectations of four-year college and university students in life sciences and other S&E programs nationwide.

Instructor and Student Questions for essay #2:

1. Based upon their openings, which article, #1 or #2, has more predictable arguments, claims, and information that will be presented?

2. Can you, to some extent, predict the structure or outline of the essay's "body"?

3. Can you predict the opinion or "findings" the closing will state?

4. What reasons would the authors have for presenting their information in these different ways?

5. How does the presentation of information change the "tone" of the piece? Is one style easier to read solely for remembering main ideas?

6. How will you know which style to choose in your own writing assignments?

Essay #3:

COLD BACON AND SPAM
By Liberty Kohn

I am Fred
I am Fred
Fred who is out of his head.

That Fred in his head.
That Fred in his head.

He does not like
cold breakfast
with the fam.
He does not like cold bacon
and spam.

I do not like them,
says I,
Fred the head.

Would I like them
up or down?

I would not like them
up or down.
I would not like them
with a clown.
I would not like them
in outer space.
I would not eat them
to win a race.
Cold bacon and spam,
side by side,
I would rather whither away,
or eat them fried.

Questions of Essay #3:

1. Is there information being distributed in this piece, or is this only nonsense?

2. Does it have an argument? Does it have an opening thesis, closing statement, etc.? Would you categorize the thesis as direct or indirect?

3. Are there types of evidence in this piece to support a thesis?

Essay #4:

Justice Thomas Carries The Day
USA TODAY
July 5, 2007 Thursday
FINAL EDITION
Tony Marou

A week has passed, yet the memory of what transpired at the Supreme Court on June 28 remains vivid.

Usually a staid and solemn place, the court produced high drama that morning as announced a landmark ruling curtailing the use of race in assigning students to one public school or another in pursuit of diversity. There was drama in what could be seen, and in what was invisible, as well.

As the court announced perhaps the most significant race case in a decade, the court's only African-American justice, was barely visible — literally. He sits next to Justice Stephen Breyer, and the two can often be seen chatting amiably. But as Breyer read his angry dissent, accusing the majority of turning its back on decades of civil rights precedents, I looked up to see how Thomas was reacting — and could not see him.

At first, I thought Thomas had left the bench. But Thomas was there, it turns out; he had just pushed his chair back so far that he was almost behind Breyer, well out of view. It was as though Thomas did not want to be seen in the same photo frame with Breyer — except, of course, photos are not allowed in the court anyway.

Thomas' invisibility on the bench was matched in the media coverage that ensued. We all wrote about the influence of Roberts and his fellow Bush-appointed newcomer, Samuel Alito, both in the majority. We focused also on Justice Anthony Kennedy, whose middle-ground concurring opinion could ultimately dictate the impact of the decision. Kennedy's opinion only highlighted the media focus on his role as the crucial swing vote on the court.

But these analyses might miss a larger point about the court, and about the influence of Justice Thomas. The court's decision on June 28 marks a cultural as well as a legal turning point on the issue of race, and conservative Thomas probably deserves more credit — or blame — than anyone has yet recognized. After 16 years on the court — often spent as invisible as he was last week — Thomas' disdain for affirmative action, and his skepticism about the value of integrated schools, carried the day.

When Thomas' predecessor, the civil rights titan Thurgood Marshall, died in 1993, his colleagues paid him tribute by talking about the power of his storytelling within the private discussions of the justices. Marshall would inject an anecdote from his youth or his days as an NAACP litigator into his conversations, giving his colleagues a steady and powerful proof that, as he often said, he never had to look at his hand to remind himself that he was black.

Questions of Essay #4:

1. Is the thesis statement here direct or indirect? Whether direct or indirect, write the thesis statement here:_____

    _____

2. How is the information presented? Is the argument presented as objective, real-world, researched information, or is the argument presented as highly personal opinion? Where can you identify passages in the essay's opening to support your answer?

3. What reading strategy works best to make sense of this essay?

4. What areas of knowledge does this piece assume of the reader?

5. What information seems secondary and of interest only to those that have background knowledge of race issues and political standing in the Supreme Court's justices?

Essay #5:

FROM FANTASY TO FAITH: MORALITY, RELIGION AND TWENTIETH-CENTURY LITERATURE

by D.Z. Phillips, 2006. London, SCM, pp. 240. ISBN 0 334 04028 0 (pbk).
Review by Liberty Kohn

When he passed in August 2006 at the age of 71, philosopher Dewi Zephaniah Phillips had garnered an international reputation for his contributions as a member of the Swansea school of philosophy. Based in Wittgenstein's moral philosophy, Phillips continually resisted ideas that morality and moral philosophy should be enmeshed in human purposes, be they humdrum human happiness or Panglossian battlelines over catastrophe and divine responsibility: Discussion of morality and faith shouldn't be bound to external justifications. Phillips questioned the limits of philosophical skepticism, in particular skeptical language's ability to address matters beyond truth-value. Although open to criticisms of Wittgensteinian fideism then and now, Phillips should be remembered as a champion of religious faith in a sometimes hostile intellectual environment, as an advocate of religious discussion without the encumbrance of its philosophical material ties, and as a proponent of literature's ability to transmit the values of both humanism and spiritual faith.

Originally released in 1991 and produced in a 2006 second edition, Phillips' *From Fantasy to Faith: Morality, Religion and Twentieth-Century Literature* is a vehicle for his continuing philosophy calling for a divorce of philosophy and theology, as well as an assessment of skepticism's effects on literature and the purposes of literary reading. Yet Phillips designed this collection around the explication of literature, twenty-one essays on twenty-one authors, allowing for discussion and exemplification of the variety of ways literary language provides a less limited discourse for discussions of faith and morality. Thus, the book is interesting because it does not read as a manifesto or tome. Phillips' critical method is in the vein of the interpretative strategy for which he argues, a secular-exegesis-returning-the-sacred-to-literature, which he provides through his rereading of literature from throughout the century.

In Part One of the book, 'Somewhere Over the Rainbow', Phillips endeavors 'to give full weight to the pervasive intellectual view in Western culture that, by now, we should have put aside the inherent childishness of religious belief' (p. x). Phillips suggests that neither intellectualism, artistic creation nor artistic appreciation can be inclusive for an entire populace, leading Phillips to looming questions: Do we need charitable untruths to get us through a turbulent life? Is religion this type of beneficial, requisite and inclusive untruth? [...]

Who, What, When, Where, Why, and How (WWWWWH)

A quick check to guarantee you have all the components of a strong thesis is asking yourself Who, What, When, Where, Why, and How. Not all of these components may fit into a single sentence definable as your thesis, but these important areas of information will almost always appear in your introductory paragraph or paragraphs. To be sure that you've included all the relevant information to your readers, you may wish to outline your subject as follows:

Who:
What:
When:
Where:
Why:
How:

If you are not solving a problem or using a methodology for your writing purpose, or writing on a topic that includes these, the "how" does not always exist. Still, you can doublecheck your basic information and its depth, guaranteeing a stronger focus for yourself and for your readers.

Let's revisit our Star Wars example:

> *Star Wars* was destined for box office success because of the nation's ongoing interest in space exploration, as well as its epic plot, which was absent from much previous science fiction.

Who: *Star Wars*
What: destined for box office success
When: late 1970s
Where: United States? the world?
Why: ongoing interest in space exploration, epic plot
How: ?

The Star Wars example demonstrates several interesting points. First, the "Who" may not be a person. The Who is the subject of your essay. It may be people, an object, an idea, or other things. However, it is the focus. Second, certain bits of information are often implied. Although the paragraph doesn't say the late 1970s, everyone knows that this is the date of *Star Wars* release and subsequent box office records. The author is trusting the audience to know the period of the movie's release. Not all subjects will be as universally known as *Star Wars*. Dates may need to be included.

Also, the "Where" is missing as well. While either The "United States" or "The World" would work, the author may want to add this information to the introduction, signaling the limits "where" that will be discussed in the essay. Also, the *how* is absent. I would suggest that here, because no problem is being solved, the *how* is absent. Or the *why* and the *how* are very similar in this case: because of an interest in space exploration and because of an epic plot. Lastly, as we shall see in the Einstein example, WWWWWH can often be refocused, reshaping your thesis and filling in missing categories.

Now let's look at our Einstein example:

> Albert Einstein's Theory of Relativity was initially rejected by the community, but not as much as some history books have claimed.

List the information from above below, also noting what is absent:

Who:

What:

When:

Where:

Why:

How:

You'll notice a fair amount of key information is absent. As a writer, you would have to decide, based upon your audience and subject, whether or not these absences will be filled in by the reader's general knowledge. I would suggest the following for our thesis on Einstein:

Who: Albert's Einstein's Theory of Relativity
What: initially rejected
When: [early twentieth century]
Where: scientific community
Why: ?
How: ?

In the above example, *Where* is not a place, but a body of people with shared knowledge. Much like *Who,* the answers to these questions might not conform to your ideas of Who, What, When, Where, Why, and How. This is because much argument is theoretical, so it takes place nowhere, so to speak. If applied and practiced, then it may take on physical features. If only hypothetical, some parts of the WWWWWH grid may not conform to your expectations.

Also, we have extra information that doesn't fit well: *but not as much as some history books have claimed.* This is because of the writing style. The "What" most likely is:

the initial rejection of the Theory of Relativity is overstated in history books

You may have noticed the *Why* behind the rejection of Einstein's Theory of Relativity is absent from this sentence. The absent information could be included somewhere else in the introductory paragraph. After all, not everything can fit into one sentence. Or it may be because our subject needed to be refocused because of our new *What.*

Who: Historians
What: overstated the initial rejection of the Theory of Relativity in history books.
When: during the Twentieth Century
Where: the world? Europe?
Why: ?
How:?

You can see how the WWWWWH grid has allowed us to refocus our first paragraph, providing the absent information. You can read the Who, What, and When and get a thesis equally strong or stronger than the initial version. The "Where" doesn't seem to have changed, and everyone knows historians are found in countries everywhere. However, as a writer, you should try to define your limits in each category. *Historians in Europe,* or *historians before the 1960s,* or whatever specific group or individual one is writing about. Also, the *why* and *how* behind the rejection of the theory seem easier to imagine now: common belief and trends in historical writing.

These are ideas that challenge the WWWWWH grid, but by using the method, you can see upcoming challenges in presenting complex information, you can detail general information, (such as missing actors, as with *historians*) and you can guarantee you have provided a beginning framework for your explanation or argument.

Identifying Argumentative Claims

Previously, we learned that arguments forward specific claims about the truth, legitimacy, or effectiveness of ideas. Any argument offering a workable solution or answer to a problem, whether scientific or philosophical, starts with a claim. Poor arguments also start with a claim, but poor arguments may be underspecified, may not solve the problem, and may lack enough support and evidence to be legitimate answers to questions.

Claims, good or poor, are statements that can be denied or affirmed. If your statement or thesis cannot be denied or confirmed, then you may only be explaining, not arguing. Statements such as "All individuals are born free," "Stem cell research is immoral," "Nurturance predicts behavior better than biology," and "Stan is a good guy" are all claims. In short, a person can argue *for* them or *against* them. Imagine evidence arguing both for and against each of the four claims just stated. If you can imagine arguments existing both for and against, you have an argument.

Claims will typically be written in the form of declarative sentences. This is undoubtedly the strongest form to state an argumentative claim. Some writers may try to state their claim through a question, but it is doubtful whether or not this is always an effective form to convince your audience. The use of the four sentence types will be discussed at length in the Chapter Four.

For Discussion: Are the following argumentative claims? Or are they only facts? For each of the above statements that is an argumentative claim, imagine evidence to both support and refute the validity of these claims. Discuss the answers as a class or in small groups.

Dogs are man's best friend.
Diamonds are a girl's best friend.
The average human head weighs eight pounds.
Natural diamonds are compressed coal.
The post-World War II Leavitt Town was the model for later American suburbs.
Leave me alone.
Germans are an efficient people.
It is easier to do good than evil.
We have not yet discovered all the elements that comprise our universe.
Peanuts is written by Charles Schultz.
Peanuts is a comic strip representing the common personality types of twentieth-century
    American life.
The sun is a star.
Not everything is a claim.
Trying times make heroes of all women and men.
Some people don't look good in warm colors.
There are sixteen ounces in a pound.

Recognizing Claims in The Classroom

Sometimes instructors may give you a claim to defend, as in the following:
    Argue that Ophelia's relationship to her father parallels Hamlet's relationship to his mother.
    Defend the claim that science and creationism can co-exist without detriment to either science or faith.

Most often you'll receive an argumentative prompt offering you a choice:

> *Discuss whether current environmental laws focusing on greenhouse emissions are firm enough to reverse global warming trends.*

> *Agree or Disagree: Freud's psychological theory is rooted not in the mysteries of the human mind, but in the anxieties of his own mind.*

> *What role does race play in class divisions in twenty-first-century America?*

The term *claim* can be viewed as simply another term for "thesis" or "proposition." Arguments have one major thesis; however, they have many claims in their network of evidence and support. And remember, argumentative claims are not a summary of an idea. Argumentative claims suggest that you "take a side" or "make a point." Arguments don't just explain an idea, event, or item: They explain how the idea, event, or item is a valid conclusion about an open-ended topic with a variety of viewpoints.

Five Forms of Argument

After you have read widely, outlined your goals for writing, and narrowed your topic, you will begin to write. Your first draft should keep audience and purpose in mind. The first draft will have a lot of excess material that will be edited. This is OK. Keep the excess material. You cannot predict which ideas you will keep, which ideas you will erase, and which ideas will be the seed for more ideas in future drafts. Upon completing the imagination and prewriting required at the beginning of the writing process, you will need to re-examine and organize your thoughts. Eventually, you will have to revise the language of these thoughts. In the early stages of writing, language can be revised, but language is not the only feature that needs to be revised. Thinking must also be revised.

Why does thinking need to be revised and re organized? Because no thought spills from our mind perfect, united, and organized. The following types of argument have been used for centuries upon centuries. Most arguments utilize more than one form at various points in a communication. Long arguments may utilize all. Because these categories are the basic modes of making sense of the world around us, it is often helpful to look at your thesis and basic support and ask which mode you are using. For further practice, you may wish to look at Chapter Nine's rough drafts and Chapter Ten's polished, final drafts, identifying the forms of argument each thesis and claim uses. Although there are many forms of argument and exposition, here are some forms common to academic argument:

Argument by Definition

Argument by Comparison and Contrast

Argument by Illustration and Example

Argument by Classification and Division

Argument by Cause and Effect

Each form has certain predictable qualities that you use everyday without realizing it. Your prewriting thesis, no matter how unformed, will contain elements of one of these forms of thought. To help you tidy up your thoughts, you may wish to ask yourself which argument your prewriting thesis most closely resembles. You are asking yourself basic questions: How am I thinking? How am I suggesting that the world works? How am I talking about a particular event or idea? What events and ideas am I surrounding the event with to give it importance?

Argument by Definition

In argument by definition, your thesis is not based upon situational solutions. Instead, you are concentrating on the qualities internal to an idea itself. You will suggest that a your subject has the qualities of a certain class of things, therefore it should be treated the same as other members of this class of things. Your argument will show why it belongs in the class it does and how other opinions have wrongly classified it, providing an incorrect solution to the problem.

You won't spend a lot of time comparing how your idea is better or worse than a similar idea. Instead, you will be arguing that the qualities of the "thing" you are promoting are highly valuable. Those who argue from definition on social issues may believe their values and solutions permanent and timeless and applicable to a variety of problems, so argument by definition typically doesn't aim for a "multiple answer" mentality to solving problems. Instead, it outlines its ideals and values, defends them, and suggests that readers would be wise to adopt these ideals and values as well.

Argument by definition entails defining the limits of your subject. You must set boundaries. Your support and claims will reinforce these boundaries of the good and the less good, the fair and the not-so-fair, the useful and the less useful, and the efficient and the inefficient. You and your thesis are walling off certain parts of the world, finding that some ideas should not be as highly valued as others. If you are arguing that democracy is the most benevolent form of government, then you are walling off other forms of government such as theocracy, communism, and monarchy. You would begin by defining the qualities of a good government. They may be

Equality of all citizens
Right to own property
Right of people to create own laws and legislative bodies
Right of people to amass wealth through hard work
Religious freedom
Social mobility

You can see that these are a few of the qualities of democracy not offered by other governmental schemas. If you argue that these are the most important values to humankind when building a government, you are arguing from definition. Abraham Lincoln often argued from definition. His most famous argument from definition was an argument over what the definition of a human being is. Why would this be important to Lincoln? Obviously, Lincoln was arguing for the Emancipation Proclamation, and he needed Americans to see not black and white, but only the human being. Arguing from definition allowed Lincoln to set up his qualities and values in such a way that neither race nor the need for cheap labor could be a valid proposition for continuing slavery. Many argument theorists suggest that definition is the strongest form of argument. Lincoln certainly thought so. He did not risk history to another form of argument. Many other "core values" arguments, typically derived from either religious principles or the United States constitution, are arguments by definition.

Argument by definition typically follows this formula: *X is a Y because it has features A, B, C, etc.* Or the following is possible: *X is not a Y because it does not have features A, B, C, etc.* It is easy to see that a hot-button issue can be argued from both conservative and liberal viewpoints through definition.

Conservative argument by definition:

Stem cell research is immoral and murderous because scientific theory denies the sanctity and preservation of all life, and the stem cell research process destroys stem cell clusters.

Liberal argument by definition:

Stem cell research is moral because science can better help those living with disabilities and illness, and the stem cell research process destroys embryos or cell clusters that will never grow into a human being.

Each of these definitions of what is moral depends upon limiting the qualities of what defines "morality." The values of each speaker are different. Thus, their definition will be different. Here are some other examples: *Video game violence is/is not equal to real violence because…Stepparents are/are not as compatible with children as biological parents because … Stealing a library book that no one has read in fifty years is/is not a crime because … Common-law marriage is/is not a marriage because …*

Syllogisms

The syllogism is an ancient device that proves methodically that one thing is the same as another. You can see why this would be useful when arguing by definition. Here is the rationale for syllogisms:

Claim: X is a Y
Reason: Because it has qualities A, B, and C
Grounds: X has certain qualities
Warrant: If something has A, B, and C, then it can be called an X
Backing: Evidence that Y has A, B, and C

Not everyone may agree that Y has qualities A, B, and C. Think of the stem cell example. The qualities of A, B, and C are different for each. Those who disagree with a viewpoint can argue either the grounds or the warrant.

Exercise:

If someone has the conservative view of stem cell research, what would they say when attacking the liberal grounds?

First, figure out what the liberal grounds are. List them.

1.
2.

Now, discuss how these grounds are different than the conservative grounds. You may wish to list the conservative grounds.

If this same person of conservative viewpoint chose to attack the liberal warrant, what specific qualities of the liberal argument would they be attacking?

For practice, you may wish to repeat this exercise from the liberal standpoint as well

Here are some examples of syllogisms. I will condense the entire syllogism into three parts and show only how X is a Y. This means that I am leaving out the qualities or reasons (A, B, C, etc.) that allow one to argue from definition. As you read these, imagine what the qualities or reasons are, and also imagine if there is any way to refute the qualities or reasons.

Major premise: All men are mortal.
Minor premise: Socrates is a man.
Conclusion: Socrates is mortal.
Major premise: Stainless steel will not rust.
Minor premise: This can is made from stainless steel.
Conclusion: This can will not rust.

Major premise:	Only politicians that are sensible are electable
Minor premise:	That politician is electable.
Conclusion:	That politician is sensible.
Major premise:	All students who graduate will get a good job.
Minor premise:	That student will graduate.
Conclusion:	That student will get a good job.

The first syllogism is the classic example of syllogisms. Are the other examples perfectly constructed and inevitable as the first? Is it possible that the syllogism can provide faulty logic as well sound logic? What is different about the fields of study covered by the last three syllogisms that does or does not guarantee their logic is flawless. Anyone who argues knows that not all claims and grounds are universal. Different people have different values. Even people with similar values will change their opinion as an idea moves from one situation to another. Stem cell research, for instance, may be murder to someone until a loved one is struck with an illness treatable through stem cell research. The situation has changed and the idea of stem cell research has a different frame—one where the good of science counts for more than it did previously. Or, even if they believe in the values behind their argument by definition, the *situation* has changed and the old values don't seem to count. Likewise, an argument to go to war may be founded upon being attacked, but what constitutes an attack may differ from situation to situation. And even then, people will either see or not see that the qualities and evidence necessitate going to war or not.

Knowing the general idea behind argument by definition can help you see if you are thinking of your topic as an idea that does not require comparison, contrast, causes, or effects to make it a viable solution or answer to a problem. The definitional idea itself applies to any related issues or conundrums. There is no cause or effect that can alter the definition's ability to provide an answer. An answer can always be made based upon the values of the definition itself.

Argument by Comparison and Contrast

Unlike argument by definition, contrasting and comparing examines both the good and bad of two distinct ideas, texts, problems, or solutions. Your own argument and solution may draw upon the good and bad of both idea A and B, or may demonstrate how idea B encapsulates idea A and goes beyond idea A, or may discredit one in favor of the other. You can always expect that you will have both an A and a B to compare and contrast, whether they are theories, texts, solutions, organizations, or people.

Comparison points out similarities. *Contrast* points out differences. You'll need similarities to prove to your audience that A and B should be discussed together. Your thesis or introductory paragraph should suggest these similarities. Yet your reasons for comparing A and B, as well as the major differences, should also appear in your thesis.

Like other types of argument, you must think critically about your subject. Discussing similarities and differences is a good start. However, you must be sure to do more than summarize when arguing. Your paper's points of comparison and contrast should be based on the particular problem you are tackling, and theses points should become your support for your solution as well.

Building Criteria

You may wish to develop a framework or graph to help you organize your criteria. It may look like the following example. The criteria are what each generally shares, yet the qualities of these criteria will vary, helping you make your decision:

Criteria:	Reading Books:	Watching TV:
Amount of time:	takes more time	takes less time
amount of information:	more information	less information
depth of information:	detailed research expected	less detail expected
ability to validate sources:	can see sources listed	some sources cited
specificity on a subject:	topics can be very specific	broad or specific
availability:	must be found ahead of time	always broadcasting

While it may look like books are the winner here, your argument for what is "best" depends upon your thesis. Here are several arguments that could use the above list:

Compare and contrast the quality and detail of information that we receive from both books and television.

Compare and contrast two types of communication, organizing your criteria to choose a medium that gives a lot of general information quickly.

Compare and contrast the ability to verify sources between two modes of communication.

These are not the only possibilities. You'll notice that some of these questions ask you to choose a "victor" after you've compared and contrasted. Others do not explicitly ask this. You should decide whether or not your purposes require a "victor." If you are arguing, naturally you must choose a position and defend it through criteria like those listed above. Often times, your criteria alone won't result in a victor; your criteria will present you with a well planned answer to a question or solution to a problem. Yet you must find support and evidence to persuade your audience the criteria are relevant and effective.

You may also notice that a list like that one above is not highly specific. Each claim, such as books making it easier to verify sources, may or may not be true. It would depend upon what type of books you are examining. Popular culture books and non-fiction can be argumentative yet written without a single source to support them. The support may simply come from the writer's own thought. This is both freeing and dangerous, argumentatively speaking. You may wish to discuss as a class both the freeing and dangerous aspects of people who argue without including the opinion of others qualified to speak on a subject. Also, you can see that the things you examine (ideas, problems, texts, people, etc.) need to be well-selected for similarities, and the criteria must be detailed enough to provide an in-depth analysis. Otherwise, the differences won't be highly relevant and won't support your position.

Your criteria can be based upon the type of things you are examining. Based on the categories I've provided, you may wish to ask the following questions to get your comparison and contrast started:

Theories (Ideas, Problems):

What are these theories about? What problem to they attempt to define or solve? Are the theories applicable in the same fields? Does each theory originate in the same historical period? Does the period of origin matter when evaluating the theory? Is your problem the same as the original problem the theory was meant to solve? How have the theories been used in the past? What types of people used them for what situations? Were they successful?

Texts and Art (print, visual, and otherwise):

What themes do these texts describe and discuss? Are these themes timeless, or are they historically-bound? Does that change the way the themes are viewed by the writer compared to modern readers? By what qualities does the text wish and deserve to be judged (style, theme, characterization, plot, writer's intention, historical importance, historical representation, etc.)?

People:

What is the origin of this person? Are there formative years (education, environment, opportunities, etc.) normal or unique? Does the journey define their later accomplishments? What are this person's values? Are they groundbreaking for the "type" of person they are (gender, race, class, religion, etc.) or for their accomplishment only?

Groups:

What is this group's origins? What was its original purpose? Has that purpose changed? What effect has the group had on the area of society they wish to affect? What is their strategy? Have the purposes or strategies had any unwanted side effects? Does the group have a recognizable political persuasion?

Recognizing Argument by Comparison and Contrast

Recognizing assignments of this type is fairly easy. The key words are typically *compare*, *contrast*, *similarities*, and *differences*. Here are some examples. Notice that both similarity and difference may not be asked for in the question, but it will be expected that you provide it to some degree.

Compare the political events surrounding President Lincoln's assassination with the political events surrounding President Kennedy's assassination.

Contrast the ways in which liberal theory and neo-conservative theory use tax revenues to support education. Argue that one provides a comprehensive educational plan.

What are the differences between the comedy of Mark Twain and the comedy of modern day sitcoms? Which one qualifies as satire?

You'll notice that the first question doesn't ask for an argument, although the second and third questions do. You may wish to ask your instructor if argument is a requirement if the assignment prompt doesn't specify this important point. The second prompt asks for an argument. The third prompt is the trickiest. It indirectly asks that you organize your differences around the criteria for "satire," yet it doesn't state so directly. If you organized your criteria for any other purpose than discovering which one is satirical, you will not have answered the second question.

Your thesis will generally contain your major findings on the differences of A and B. Often, your thesis will contain the brief similarity as well.

Example Thesis

While both liberal and neo-conservative educational plans provide a comprehensive educational plan for all American schoolchildren, the neo-conservative plan to offer school vouchers and privatize education offers choice and quality in education that the liberal plan cannot provide.

Example Thesis

While neo-conservative educational plans provide more choice to some American families, the voluntary segregation and unequal funding of public schools that would result from privatization are not part of the democratic ideals or equal opportunity upon which America is based; only liberal theory guarantees higher learning rooted in American democracy's ideals.

You can easily spot both A and B, liberal and conservative viewpoints, in these sample theses, despite slightly different approaches to presenting the information in each.

Organizing Your Essay

Most comparison and contrast essays work from similar structures. You can either present idea A first in its entirety, evaluating it point-by-point. Afterward, you present idea B point-by-point in its entirety.

The second method of organization is to evaluate idea A by one point, then evaluate idea B by the same point. This method offers an instant comparison for the reader, but it offers only parts without giving the audience a whole A or B. You will have to decide which method is best for your assignment. Here are some questions to help you decide:

1. Will people forget a point-by-point analysis too easily because of a large amount of information?

2. Depending on how familiar with the topic and ideas my audience is, how much do I need to explain A and B as separate whole entities before dissecting them into parts?

3. Which type of comparison/contrast essay allows me to illustrate and support my thesis and argument quickly?

4. Which type of organization allows me to most easily demonstrate how my immediate claim and contrast relate to my thesis?

As you can see from the questions, your audience's familiarity with your subject is important to your organization, as is the ability to quickly show important differences' relevance to your thesis. Remember that these "differences" will often rely on previous comparison and contrast—this is where organization becomes important in comparison/contrast essays. No essay is mathematically organized from beginning to end. Although discussing only idea A then idea B, or discussing each criterion point-by-point would be organizationally perfect, you may have to break out of either pattern at times to relate details to your argument.

Comparing and contrasting is a basic mode of thought. We all make choices everyday based on a better/worse scale. Comparing and contrasting can help you build criteria to support for your prewriting ideas, and it can help you continue to think of related material. Even if you don't choose to argue by comparison and contrast, you'll add to your prewriting ideas by thinking with this method.

Argument by Illustration or Example

Argument by illustration is a unique form of argument that provides a "story" of sorts to argue why something works well. If you are arguing about how a professional sports team should be managed, you may use the story of a championship team to illustrate the finer points of managerial strategy. Your "story," however, is not just a story of victories, great plays, and game-by-game analysis. Your illustration would cover all the criteria of other forms of argument that are less "story" driven. For example, the managerial strategies for a sports team would probably include argument about how to choose a coach, the coach's relationship with management, how to draft players, how to construct a team identity, etc.

The "story" of how you were elected class president would contain a blueprint on how to self-nominate, campaign, communicate your views, and debate an opponent.

While each of these would be told as part of the "story" of the championship season, each part of the story would serve as an example of how a team should be run. This means you would analyze and abstract certain principles from the story that could be used as advice for any coach of a sports team. These abstractions are the argumentative structure. The story of the team is one form of support. Although it may not matter how you arrive at these abstract lessons on how to manage a sports team, it is these abstractions that make your story more than just an inspiring story.

You will also need sources for your argument. These will typically work in support of the abstractions from your argument.

Exercise: The following could be passages from the story of a championship season in the making. Write an abstract principle below each.

1. Coach Bruce Smith was a man destined for Super Bowl greatness. As a player, he won two MVP awards and back-to-back Super Bowls. As a college coach, his team ranked in the Top Ten eleven out of his fifteen years.

2. While an assistant coach in the NFL, Coach Smith worked closely with general manager Avery Shield, trading advice and recruiting strategies.

3. Coach Smith personally talked to and recruited Tom Johnson and D.D. Tavrick, his star wide receiver and quarterback.

4. During the years leading up to the championship season, Coach Smith dismissed an All-Pro tight end, Chuck Bearweather, for consistently being late for practice. He also dismissed a kick returner Jim Shackford for publicly criticizing the return coverage during the preseason.

5. Although his top three recruits did not display much promise two years ago, Coach Smith gave these players assignments on special teams. All three of these draftees started during the championship season, and one was nominated All-Pro. All three have signed contracts for another three years, despite offers from other clubs.

Potential Answers:

1. Players who are successful as professional players and college coaches will be good professional coaches.

2. A football team with a coach and management that cooperate and share ideas may increase their chances of a successful season.

3. Coaches who have personal contact with potential players will have a better chance of signing those players.

4. Dismissing players who are undisciplined or critical may help team cohesion.

5. Developing rather than dismissing developing players can lead to their better play and a dedication to the team rather than money and free agency.

Each of these are argumentative claims that could work in other forms of argument as well. Abstracting these from the "story" allows you to support them with similar opinions from secondary sources—in this case, secondary sources on management and leadership in professional sports and perhaps management in general. Many of the student essays in the final chapter of this book are argument by illustration. Look to these for examples of how a story provides an argumentative structure.

Because illustration represents the natural "stories" of life, it can be very helpful for extending your prewriting thoughts. Imagining how your topic fits into the story of your life or others' lives can help you use your life experience to discover ideas that may never enter your mind while making abstract lists.

Argument by Classification and Division

The purpose of argument by classification and division is to create categories that explain your problem and/or your solution. Classifying your problem or solution can help to explain differences to both yourself and your audience. These differences can go beyond explanation into argument in a variety of ways. After classifying the problem different ways, you can offer a solution that solves each class of problem. You would most likely engage each problem with your solution in separate paragraphs, but not necessarily so.

Classification and division allows you to solidly and predictably *order* your topic, problems, and solutions. While some essays are a mosaic or weave of claims, support, and counterargument with a unique and unpredictable order, classification often visually presents its contents with subject headings for each problem or solution.

Your problems, once classified, should not overlap. Creating clear cut categories is a hallmark of this type of argument. When categories creating a problem are fuzzy, as they often are in life, argument by classification and division may not be the right choice to communicate or persuade. However, this type of argument can potentially help you distinguish and limit fuzzy categories, making them clearer.

As always, your essay will need a thesis. This thesis may list all the categories and their solution, or it may discuss just the problem and solution generally.

While the infrastructural problems of America divide neatly into bridges, interstates, water pipes, and sewer pipes, the allotting of government funds for repair cannot be divided so neatly due to the level of disrepair for each category.

An essay of this type often has headings after the introduction:

BRIDGES

A government report suggests that all the bridges of America are in need of repair. The report found that bridges built before 1960 are architecturally less sound, yet corrosion levels and structural stress are higher than recommended on a majority of bridges built before 1980.....

INTERSTATES

A majority of state and federal analyses of interstates found that although the roads are in disrepair, they do not pose excessive danger to drivers. Furthermore, funding for these highly visible problems is consistent with federal estimates.....

It is easy to imagine the rest of the essay. It is also easy to imagine several ways to communicate the solutions. First, you could reach conclusions on the urgency of particular classes' disrepair. Then, using the same headings as the first half of your essay, you could provide solutions. This format may work well with some essays. However, you would be separating your solution from the in-depth explanation of the problem. Thus, providing a solution immediately following each problem's description may be more appropriate and easier on your reader's memory and understanding.

Two Outline Strategies for Classification and Division

Outline One:

 I. Introduction/Thesis
II. Problems
    A. Bridges
    B. Interstates
    C. Water Pipes
    D. Sewer Pipes
III. Solutions
    A. Bridges
    B. Interstates
    C. Water Pipes
    D. Sewer Pipes
IV. Conclusion

Outline Two:

I. Introduction/Thesis
II. Classifications
    A. Bridges
        a) problems
        b) solutions
    B. Interstates
        a) problems
        b) solutions
    C. Water Pipes
        a) problems
        b) solutions
    D. Sewer Pipes
        a) problems
        b) solutions
III. Conclusion

    Arguments by classification and division can be useful when you have a wealth of information but are not sure how to organize it. Separating your material into classes can help you see which strands of information, ideas, problems, and solutions belong together. Even if you choose not to argue through definition and classification, the process of classifying your prewriting thoughts and any research will help you organize information for any type of essay.

Argument by Cause and Effect

Cause and effect arguments explain the reasons or results of an event, idea, or situation. This mode of communication will also work well for explanation. Whether or not you have an argument will depend on whether or not your causes or effects are opinions rather than facts. If your thesis is an opinion, not fact, then even if you use facts as causes or effects, they are working in service of your opinion. Contentious scientific issues such as global warming, deforestation, and stem-cell research are examples of scientific fact used in the service of a values-laden argument. Cause and effect can also be used for cultural "values" argument as well, where causes and effects are hypothetical.

    There are three basic types of cause and effect arguments: multiple causes/one effect, one cause/multiple effects, and chain or domino effect.

    The multiple causes/one effect can be organized as follows:

Thesis: *American children are not being protected from dangerous Chinese toys for three reasons: lack of Chinese governmental oversight, lack of U.S. testing on Chinese imports, and lack of U.S. trade penalties against China for lax toy safety laws.*

Three Outline Strategies for Cause and Effect

This essay could easily be organized in the following manner:

I. Introduction/Thesis
II. Lack of Chinese Governmental Oversight
    a) reason/cause
    b) reason/cause

III. Lack of U.S. Testing
    a) reason/cause
    b) reason/cause
IV. Lack of U.S. trade penalties against China
    a) reason/cause
    b) reason/cause
  V. Conclusion

The one cause/multiple effects will be similar to the following. Fill in any gaps left in the outline:

Obesity is one of the major problems facing Americans today. It can result in physical and mental health problems, as well as removal from an active lifestyle.

  I. Introduction/Thesis
 II. Physical Health Problems
    a)
    b)
    c)
III. Mental Health Problems
    a)
    b)
IV. Removal From an Active Lifestyle
    a)
    b)
  V. Conclusion

The third type of cause and effect argument is a chain effect, also known as a domino effect. The above argument against obesity could be easily organized as a domino effect.
    Write a thesis for the simple outline below:
  I.

 II. Obesity has been linked to physical health problems such as
    a) high blood pressure
    b) diabetes
    c) shortness of breath
III. Physical symptoms can inhibit an active lifestyle
    a) less endorphins in bloodstream
    b) accelerates the body's aging process
IV. The inactive lifestyle can result in
    a) low self-esteem
    b) mild depression
    c) lack of sexual drive
  V. Conclusion

The above example of the cause/domino effect demonstrates the *potential* effects of a cause. They are not guaranteed. You may wish to think about what fields deal in absolute domino effects and which fields have only the potential for various domino effects.

Exercise: Identifying Argument: Which type of argument is the following thesis and outline?

Twenty-four hour TV news channels distort or omit important information required for a full discussion of current events and politics.

    I. Reporting Distorts Information
        a) Hosts have political bias
        b) Station owners have political bias
    II. Medium Distorts Information
        a) argument, not cooperation, encouraged
        b) extremist views encouraged
        c) entertainment valued over neutral information
    III. Medium Omits Information
        a) Two minute stories lack detail
        b) Point-counterpoint format not used

Each of the above is a cause. The effect is the misrepresentation of current events by cable news shows. This claim is argumentative. Some of the support for these claims may be data or surveys. Others may merely be opinion. Also, you may see that certain sections have more causes than others. Also, some causes may be placed under a variety of areas. This is OK. Not all causes and effects can be easily categorized.

As with other forms or argument, cause and effect may be a good organizing strategy for your prewriting. Gathering together a cause for each effect may help you see what information belongs together. If you find a cause with no effect or vice-versa, you can fill in what is most likely a gap in your original prewriting.

Out of the Dark

Many times we have an abundance of information but are unsure how the information relates or how to order it in an essay. The focus of this chapter was to demonstrate not only forms of argument that many essays follow, but to demonstrate how forms of argument can shape your incomplete prewriting thoughts. Putting your early thoughts into these "containers" will help you extend your thought and fill in gaps. It may also help you choose a form that best communicates your information to your audience clearly.

SECTION 4

Wet Clay Language

❊

Playing With Information

Writing requires mastery of all those components of grammar and language usage you've developed over your lifetime and during your formal education. While speaking and writing differ in their formality, the basic "mechanics" of language do not. Beyond performing these skills correctly in a variety of levels of formality, having terminology to discuss writing will help you articulate to yourself and to others both successful and less successful moments in communication. The following sections contain exercises. However, you'll notice not all the parts of speech are included. Instead, this section focuses on some areas of sentence writing where specificity is sometimes lost. To simplify, we'll discuss nouns, verbs, and clauses as tools to build good writing.

This is not a chapter of "grammar exercises." This chapter provides tools to judge drafts and to discuss the mechanics of successful and incomplete writing. I've based each usage problem on errors I often see in my own students' writing. Please remember that the advice in this section pertains mainly to sentences. Although all this chapter's advice will be highly useful in the upcoming section on revising paragraphs and essays, the demands of combining ideas into paragraphs may override the "easier" fixes for sentences provided in this chapter. As always, you must remember your larger writing purposes, even when focusing on something as small as editing a sentence.

Instructors: There is an abundance of material in this section. You may wish to teach these sentence revision tips in a different order than I've provided here. Also, you may wish to have students try the exercises included here on their own sentences and paragraphs for further practice. Last, many exercises in this chapter can have a variety of answers. Instructors, encourage your students to share answers different than those included. Students, remember that many of these exercises do not have easily discernable right or wrong answers. Instructors and students should discuss the *quality* of all student answers.

Information or No Information? Content Words Versus Function Words:

Some words carry the ideas in language. They are called content words. Typically they are nouns, verbs, adverbs, and adjectives. Function words are more like glue. You'll need prepositions, conjunctions, and other grammatical categories to connect your content words.

When errors occur in writing that are not thought-based, but are language errors, it is often times because a writer has good ideas and content words but has glued them together wrong. Typically, when a writer is unsure how to connect two ideas, they pour on the function words hoping that enough of them will act like grammatical glue. However, extra function words nod to different relationships between your content words. Your reader becomes confused.

My program for writing includes concentrating on these content words—mainly nouns, verbs, and phrases and clauses which contain nouns and verbs, although adjectives and adverbs can be important too.

Here are several examples. Circle the information that must remain, despite the order of the information:

Ford Motor Company supports the economy of many Michigan cities.

We must prepare our youth for the future. Technology is important to the lives of teenagers, whether in school or in recreational activities.

Here are the sentences again with the information moved around. Once again, underline the words or phrases carrying information.

The economy of many Michigan cities is supported by the Ford Motor Company.

Many Michigan cities' economy is supported by the Ford Motor Company.

Support for many Michigan cities economy is provided by the Ford Motor Company.

In the above examples, what words disappear or are replaced?

They are function words. Rearranging important information means different words are needed to glue the information back together.

Try writing the "Michigan" sentences with some information missing. Does the meaning change?

1.

2.

3.

Here are some examples of lost information. How has the meaning changed?

The economy of Michigan cities is supported by the Ford Motor Company.

Michigan is supported by the Ford Motor Company.

The Ford Motor company supports Michigan.

Although the changes are small, leaving out a information like "many" or "cities" changes the precision of the sentence. Suggesting that the entire state of Michigan is supported by Ford Motors is not the precise meaning of the original sentence. However, as long as *all* the information is present, it can be arranged different ways.

Now rewrite the "teenager" sentences.

Technology is important to the lives of teenagers, whether in school or in recreational activities.

1.

2.

Now rewrite without one piece of important information. Does the sentence's meaning change?

1.

2.

3.

Here are some potential rewrites with all information included:

Whether teenagers are in school or recreational activities, technology is important to their lives.

Teenagers lives depend upon technology, whether in school or in recreational activities.

Examine these examples of small omissions of information. Has the original idea been changed?

1. Technology is important to teenagers, whether in school or recreational activities.

2. Technology is important, whether in school or recreational activities.

3. In school, technology is important in teenagers' lives.

4. Technology, whether in school or recreational activities, is important to teenager's lives.

In #1, the sentence may now imply that the technology is important to teenagers themselves, not to their life and development after their teenage years.

In #2, we don't know to *whom* the technology is important. It would include *anyone* in school or recreational activities. We've lost our subject: teenagers.

In #3, the idea of technology being important outside of school no longer exists.

In #4, some readers may see no change. Technically, it is now the *technology* that is in school and recreational activities, not the teenagers. In the original, the teenagers were in school and recreational activities.

The focus of this chapter is to teach an awareness of the ability to shift language and to recognize the content/information of all sentences. When rewriting, recognizing important information allows you to clear away non-essential information as well as change the order of information without losing the meaning. This is the path to clear sentences.

Instructors: Although passive and active voice does not appear until the "Verbs" section, you may wish to assign and discuss it here. Passive and active voice is the most obvious and traditional discussion about rearranging information.

Grammar Lessons of Old:

You undoubtedly remember being drilled on subjects, verbs, and objects in your previous schooling. Let's briefly look at the basics of a sentence. This will give us the mechanical terminology for the upcoming chapter which will focus on nouns, verbs, and clauses as the basic units of revision.

Subject:	Verb:	Object or Clause (Optional):
(Nouns)		(Noun : String of words)
The sprinter	*sprints.*	
The sprinter	*left*	*the starting line.* (object)
The sprinter	*ran*	*to the stadium.* (clause)
The president	*announced*	*the end of his bid for a second presidential term.* (object + clauses)

Nouns:

We all know what nouns are. Nouns are typically defined as a person, place, thing or idea. This definition captures the vast amount of *things* in the world, which is what nouns are. From *George*

Washington to *Smallville* to *gunnysack* to *democracy*, nouns can be concrete things a child can name, or nouns can be abstract ideas that require years of study to understand to their full extent. Nouns can be objects in a sentence, subjects in a sentence, or attached to either of these ideas as part of a longer modifying clause.

> *The <u>president</u> (subject) announced the <u>end</u> (object) of his <u>bid</u> (modifying information) for a second presidential <u>term</u> (modifying information).*

Perhaps a second definition of a noun can be found in its basic qualities. First, a noun is something that can take a "determiner." The most typical determiners are articles (a, an, the), but there are others as well. Second, nouns are conjugated as singular or plural. Most singular nouns are pluralized with -s or -es, but a noun such as *geese* complicates the singular/plural distinction. Also, mass nouns such as *sugar, sand,* and *air* are not singular, yet they are not merely singular units with an -s or -es. When awkward or unclear sentences are caused by misuse of a noun, the misuse can usually be traced to either conjugation problems or to a "missing" noun.

Exercise A. Identify the nouns in the following sentences, but more importantly, note where and how nouns can appear in a sentence (subject, object, or as part of a clause).

1. The governor of California has been sick for some time.
2. In the morning hours, I like to quietly walk around the town.
3. I prefer to eat my large meals in the evening.
4. The springtime is Uncle Ray's time.
5. Johnny went running around the town during the holiday weekend.
6. Wisconsin joined the United States in 1848.
7. Blink Theory suggests that in advertisements the quantity of exposure is more important than the quality of exposure.
8. Experts agree that the twentieth-century identity depends in large part on images normalized by society.

Conjugation Errors:

Conjugation problems have as much to do with nouns as verbs. Examine the following sentences for errors. Errors of the first several sentences are easy to spot.

> *John go to the store.*

> *The lawyer attribute his victory to inductive reasoning.*

> *Men and women around the world celebrates Arbor Day every spring.*

Conjugation errors such as these catch your eye and ear immediately. They are easily fixed by reading your paper out loud to a friend or classmate or by having your paper read to you. The next several examples are less obvious. While English teachers may catch the following errors, many others may not. It is debatable whether or not these conjugation errors impede communication. Still, some readers will spot these errors and you may lose some of your authority as a writer. The following examples have similar errors to the previous sentences, but the following errors are less obvious. Why?

The space race was sped up by the Cold War. This led to moon landings, which was in the late 60s.
Half of the crowd are in the stands, and the other half remain at the food stands.
Johnson and Johnson, a company always increasing its marketability, remain profitable to this day.

The conjugation errors here revolve around the singular or plural subject, but the "singular"ness or "plural"ness of the subject is lost because of the longer sentences. Our "ear" fails us because of all the information we have to take in and because of the long break between the subject and verb. Yet good writing will require attention to conjugation. The easiest way to deal with verbs in this situation is to make the sentence as simple as possible. This extremely simple form of the sentence is sometimes called the "kernel" sentence. By temporarily editing out extra information, you can bring the subject and verb together.

Introducing the Kernel Sentence:

In my own experience, I've found that the important of kernel sentences goes beyond conjugation. Many other errors in complex sentences can be fixed by using the kernel sentence analysis that is the focus of the next sections of this chapter. If you have a complex or compound sentence that is awkward and you can't figure out how to fix the sentence, try using less words, at least temporarily. Although you will lose information, you can add it later. Also, this formula will allow you to see what complex clause in the sentence is causing your problems, so your problems are less mysterious.

For the first example, leave out the first sentence entirely. The extra information can only subtract from your focus on the mechanics of a single sentence. You will be left with the following sentence.

This led to the moon landings, which was in the late 60s.

Now make a simpler sentence based in subject-verb-object form. The easiest way to do this is to focus on nouns and verbs.

The moon landings / was / in the late 60s.

It is now easy to let your ear or eyes catch the mistake. The wrong verb conjugation is no longer buried by all the other information. Keep in mind that this wrong verb was "buried" in a small amount of information. If you were reading or proofreading an entire paragraph, it would be even easier to pass through this mistake. This is the reason that small errors like this persist in everyone's writing. The best strategy is to identify long sentences in your writing, or complex sentences with lots of commas and clauses, and break them into their simpler form. While the essence of good writing is a mix of long and short sentences, you will need a strategy to catch simple errors as you progress into longer and more complex sentences as a writer. As you develop as a writer, this process will be more automatic and "in your head," so you will need a pen and paper less and less when rewriting. You will quickly rewrite your sentence as:

This led to the moon landings, which were in the late 60s.

We have not yet left behind nouns, yet I would like to begin a discussion of clauses as well. While your main verb can't disappear from a sentence without "killing" the sentence, nouns and clauses can disappear and leave a kernel sentence. Meaning may change, but the sentence can still function. For this reason, all of the following sections until "Verbs" will be a mixture of nouns and clauses. I believe the rules for shifting and editing their information is similar, or at least they make the rules and purposes of the verb unique, and we will deal with these two similar categories before the unique functions of the verb.

Identifying Multiple Kernels: Clauses

Clauses are "half sentences" or "fragments" that may or may not contain all the parts of a sentence. While complete sentences are known as *independent clauses*, the clauses I refer to are *dependent clauses*. These clauses typically modify a complete sentence. They can appear before, after, or in the middle of a kernel sentence. Clauses can modify a whole sentence or only part of a sentence.

Here are some complex sentences with a lot of information added through modifying clauses. Some of these sentences have conjugation errors. Some do not. Break each into its simplest kernel sentence to find potential conjugation errors.

1. While Koresh and his clan hunkered down in the compound, their stockpiled weapons piled around them, the ATF agents surrounded the premises.

To break each of these into its kernel sentence, you must first identity which clause is a full sentence.

1a. While Koresh and his clan hunkered down in the compound

1b. their stockpiled weapons around them

1c. the ATF agents surrounded the premises.

The kernel sentence is 1c. It has a subject, verb, and object. Sections 1a and 1b are simply clauses that give extra information. They do not have complete subject/verb/object or subject/verb components. By breaking the sentence down, we can see that none of the clauses have an error. Try finding the clauses and kernel sentence in the following:

2. The entire Nixon administration, its young staff famous for intellect and energy, still remain criminal in the minds of many Americans.

Again, break these into clauses.

2a. The entire Nixon administration

2b. its young staff famous for intellect and energy,

2c. still remain criminal in the minds of many Americans

None of these three parts has a subject/verb/object in one clause. So the subject is in one sentence, and the verb and object must be in another. If you read 2a and 2b together, you do not get a complete sentence. If you read 2b and 2c together, you do not get a complete sentence. If you read 2a and 2c together, you get a complete sentence:

The entire Nixon administration still remain criminal in the minds of many Americans.

Now, cross out the adverbs, adjectives and other "extras" in the sentence above. Keep only the nouns and verbs. We will see if there are any conjugation errors in the stretched out conjugation of this sentence.

Kernel sentence: The <u>administration</u> <u>remain</u> <u>criminal</u>.

Even a seemingly important modifier like *Nixon* can get in the way. So boil down things all the way. Now, you can see the conjugation is incorrect. The simple sentence should read

The administration remains criminal.

The conjugation should be the same for the longer sentence. After all, adjectives, adverbs, and clauses don't have a bearing on subject/verb conjugation.

The entire Nixon administration still remains criminal in the minds of many Americans.

Finish the third example:

Jane Addams and her Hull House compatriots stokes the fires of feminism today.

| Subject plus any extra information | Verb | Object plus any extra informatio |
| Kernel subject(noun) | Verb | Kernel object (noun) |

Is the conjugation correct?
(No. It is not. After finishing the exercise, you'll find the sentence has a compound subject.)

So we see that choosing important information while losing temporarily unimportant information (adjectives, adverbs, modifying clauses) can straighten out many conjugation problems and other problems as well. Also, many of my past students have taken to the idea that the most important "thoughts" or "information" in a sentence reside in nouns, verbs, and clauses. Being able to divide a sentence into each of these will enable you to rearrange and edit your work concisely. Why? Being able to identify nouns, verbs, and clauses as *meaningful units* of information allows you to see the "trees" instead of just the "forest."

Kernel Sentences and Sentence Combining:

Kernel sentences are also useful to gain an awareness of building complex sentences from several simpler sentences. But before we begin combining sentences, let's examine kernel sentences a bit more.

Subject	Verb/Verb phrase
Birds	*fly.*
John	*walked.*
The family	*will eat.*
That kid	*yells.*
Superman	*rules.*

These subject/verb sentences are the simplest in the English language. Because the ideas of each are simple, so is their form. Many sentences, especially in academic and formal writing, will require more information. Look at what happens when I put a complex entity into the subject slot and try to imagine using a verb with no phrase after it.

The government	*predicted*
	announced
	shifted
	situated
	will not tolerate
	withdrew

Each of the verbs accompanying government requires more information. Why? It is not just these verbs that demand more information. The government itself does such complex things that an "object" or "complement" is almost always required. If you look at verbs like "fly," "walked," and "eat," they are all simple actions. None of them have one entity, the subject, acting on another. Most college and professional writing will involve complex relationships, so the verbs you naturally choose will lead to objects. These verbs needing objects lead to other modifying phrases (requiring commas) that in turn lead to longer sentences. It is easy to see why small mistakes can appear in longer sentences and why sentences can become too long in the first place.

The government	predicted	a windfall of tax relief for the poor.
	announced	the closing of five overseas military bases.
	shifted	its stance in the war on drugs.
	situated	the problem as economic, not environmental.
	will not tolerate	states with weak drunk driving laws.
	withdrew	its support of the rebel leader.

Again, note how each of these verbs requires a noun afterward. Also note that this noun has attached to it more information that makes the sentence as specific as possible. The extra information is almost always "glued" with a preposition (of, in, with, from, etc,) after the object noun.

Subject/Doer	Verb	Object	Modifying Information
The government	predicted	a windfall	of tax relief for the poor.
	announced	the closing	of five overseas military bases.
	shifted	its stance	in the war on drugs.
	situated	the problem	as economic, not environmental.
	will not tolerate	states	with weak drunk driving laws.
	withdrew	its support	of the rebel leader.

We combine information to get rid of redundant words. It is the extra, modifying information that often finds its way into a separate sentence when it can easily be included in one sentence.

The government predicted <u>a windfall</u>. <u>This windfall</u> is comprised of tax relief for the middle class.

The government announced <u>a closing</u>. <u>The closing</u> is of five overseas military bases.

Even from only these two examples, you should see a pattern developing. The pattern is one of repeated terms. Repeated terms in close proximity are often a signal for a chance to combine your ideas into one longer yet smooth sentence.

Finish breaking the final four examples into two sentences.

The government shifted .....

The government situated .....

The government will not tolerate ....

The government withdrew ....

Another basic idea behind sentence combination is tougher to spot. It is when a verb, such as *do*, is used to replace or repeat previous information. Here is an example.

John fixes cars. Mike does that too.

We have two identical kernel sentences:

John fixes cars.

Mike fixes cars (too).

Although combination isn't visible, sentences with repeated information should be nominated for sentence combination. Here is another example.

The United States will donate twelve million dollars to refugees in Africa. Canada will donate that much too.

becomes:

The United States and Canada will donate twelve million dollars each to refugees in Africa.

As always, larger concerns such as paragraphing, style, and communication will decide whether or not to combine sentences. The main goal is to *recognize the opportunity* to combine sentences, even if you choose not to do so.

Exercise B: Combine the following sentences if possible. Some will not combine as predictably as others.

1. In terms of reciprocity, Chinese environmental policy is an ecological tragedy. This tragedy is played out everyday in weather patterns. These weather patterns are those of neighboring countries.

2. Baseball's steroid policy contramands values. These values are the values of America today and baseball's past as well.

3. While the Marshall Plan did not cure Europe immediately, Europe made a comeback. This comeback took only several decades.

4. Initial investigations suggested that the senator was guilty of embezzlement. The misappropriation of funds was the subject of the investigations.

5. Half time employees protested for adequate health care; this health care consisted of dental care and fair deductibles.

6. The scientific community declared that many minerals found on earth are found in the rest of the galaxy. These minerals predate earth's formation.

7. Television changed American society forever. Radio did that too.

8. The helicopter was first used as a weapon in Vietnam. This goes for the M-16 as well.

9. The jury debated for two hours, then they voted, and did that two more times before reaching a verdict.

Authorial Redundancy: Introducing A Sentence

Adjectives specify the quality of a noun. Adverbs specify the quality of an adverb, an adjective, or a verb. In speaking and writing, we often structure our sentences with an unnecessary use of each. Each of these grammatical categories are not part of a kernel sentence. Often times, we use adverb structures to get our sentences started, but closer analysis reveals no information exists in this "start" of the sentence.

In my opinion, cultural artifacts must be preserved at all costs.

becomes:

Cultural artifacts must be preserved at all costs.

In my opinion is not necessary. The sentence itself reveals the author's opinion, and readers understand this to be an opinion. A similar redundancy provides information that the author thought about the information in the kernel sentence, which is also true without the author stating it. One cannot have an opinion unless one has thought of it. A slightly different form of redundancy provides information on an event's happening that is already present in the verb tense. Each of these forms exist in the following exercises.

Exercise C: Edit any phrases or information that are redundant. You may wish to identify the kernel sentence to identify redundant information.

1. In the past, mercantilism has often existed in societies that traded internationally.

2. Upon looking very deeply, high school sports, the issue at hand, foster responsibility and build self-esteem.

3. By investigating steroid use in teens, I found that teens are often influenced to use steroids for better performance because their professional role models use them.

4. In light of the fact people are addicted to oil, we must investigate alternative fuel sources.

5. In my estimation of these facts, agricultural growth cannot sustain population growth.

6. Many specialists agree that energy efficient light bulbs and unplugged appliances will go a long way toward making us people who find they prioritize through a green value system.

Other Forms of Redundancy:

Redundancy can come in many forms. We already discussed repeated terms across sentences and phrases of "an author thinking aloud." Changing longer modifying phrases into a single term is sometimes a possibility as well. Look at each of the following examples. Where does the extra information typically appear? Is it a noun, verb, or phrase? Which of these substitutes for it and makes the sentence briefer?

Bill's need to run everyday has helped him regain his health.
Running everyday has helped Bill regain his health.

The company's restructuring of their employee's schedules improved productivity.
Restructuring the employee schedules improved [the company's] productivity.

My brother's having a mind of his own made a decision to sell the stock earlier than I wanted was a mistake.

My brother's decision to sell the stock earlier than I wanted was a mistake.
Having a mind of his own, my brother's decision to sell the stock earlier than I wanted was a mistake.

Exercise D: The following set of sentences has potentially empty information similar to the examples above. Rewrite the following opinion-based sentences without the authors' redundant signaling of their opinion or thoughts. Rewrite other sentences that use prepositions (to, of, etc.) to "glue" information to a noun. While none of these sentences can be considered "wrong," rewriting these sentences may move out of the subject-verb-object sentence pattern, which is good for your style.

1. My decision to acknowledge my learning disability guaranteed me the help I needed for college success.

2. My option of choosing has brought me to choose marketing as a career providing quality time and a livable salary.

3. When I think about this most of my thoughts pertain to my ideas about how melting ice caps will present a danger to coastal cities within twenty years.

4. I believe whoever commits a crime should be punished.

Exercise E: Rewrite long clauses in the following sentences into a less wordy modifier. Also, look for patterns that create these long modifying clauses.

1. The inconsistencies of the Brooks' commission was found unforgivable by those in the majority of the public opinion.

2. Non-curvilinear buildings are sores to the eyes.

3. To investigate late-nineteenth-century crime, I used the methodology of Sherlock Holmes.

4. The assassinations of the KGB agent were classified within the archives of the Russians that recorded trips to China and Cuba during the late 1940s.

5. The agency then gave an offering of one million dollars to compensate for the breaking of the law.

6. Pundits made a forecast on the economy for the year and the year after that and for each month of each year too.

Turning Two Kernels into a Complex Sentence:

Combining sentences like those above streamlines similar information for your reader. Turning short sentences into clauses and combining them with another full sentence can also enhance your style and help your reader.

> Example: *The criminal stole the candlestick. Next, the criminal leapt out of the window.*
> *After the criminal stole the candlestick, he leapt out of the window.*
> *After stealing the candlestick, the criminal leapt out of the window.*
> *My father golfed on Sunday. He was badly sunburned.*
> *While my father golfed on Sunday, he was badly sunburned.*
> *Golfing on Sunday, my father was badly sunburned.*

Notice that we often speak and write without including the "doer" in the opening clause. When combining sentences, attempt to keep a "doer" in both clauses.

Exercise F: Turn the first sentence into an introductory clause/modifying information, and combine it with the second full sentence. Remember that the "doer" must appear in the opening modifying clause.

1.   Jerry told his boss he quit. His girlfriend waited in the car.
2.   He relented to pressure to step down from office. The dictator resigned from his lifelong post.
3.   The clergy announced a fundraiser. They first held a carwash. Then they held a booksale.
4.   He turned red in the face. He called an ambulance and waited to be taken to the hospital.

   Now, rewrite each of the previous sentences (1-4) with the second sentence as an introductory clause, and the first sentence as the kernel sentence. Notice this may change the sequence of events shared by the sentences. Which examples no longer make sense when reversed?

5.

6.

7.

8.

   Now, let's look at an example of a complex combined sentences we saw earlier. Turn each of these clauses into its own sentence, rather than a fragment. You will have to change, add, or edit some words in the sentence, but you shouldn't have to modify the order of the words.

1.   While Koresh and his clan hunkered down in the compound, their stockpiled weapons piled around them, the ATF agents surrounded the premises.

   1a.
   1b.
   1c.
   If you have done this exercise correctly, you'll notice that 1a and 1b have the same subject. Repetition over sentences always signals the possibility of combining sentences. 1a and 1b could be a sentence on its own.

   Koresh and his clan hunkered down in the compound. _They_ stockpiled their weapons around them.

   becomes

1) Koresh and his clan hunkered down in the compound, their weapons stockpiled around them.
2) Koresh and his clan hunkered down in the compound, stockpiling their weapons around them.
3) Koresh and his clan stockpiled their weapons and hunkered down in the compound.

For stylistic effect, you can switch the clauses at the end.

Their weapons stockpiled around them, Koresh and his clan hunkered down.
Stockpiling their weapons around them, Koresh and his clan hunkered down.

Returning to our full sentence, I pose a question: How is it that these two complete ideas become the extra information in a kernel sentence about ATF agents surrounding the premises?

Ask yourself:

1. What grammatical features in the original sentence make the two clauses on Koresh "extra" information, rather than kernel information?

2. What is the relationship between the kernel information and the extra information and the real-world actions the writer wishes to express?

Sentence Modeling:

A great way to vary your sentence types is to practice putting the same information into various positions. Our earlier clause exercises gave you the basic ability to shift information. Now apply that not only to correct errors, but to have a style that is a mix of long and short sentences.

Exercise G: Break the following sentences into clauses, as in 1a-1c above: *Trying to break the record, the man ran a mile, but failed to do so in under four minutes.*
a.
b.
c.
Next, you could turn each into its own sentence. Notice you need the kernel sentence's information to complete these other sentences.

The man tried to break the record for running a mile.
The man ran a mile.
The man failed to run a mile in under four minutes.

Notice how the repeated subject allowed for three simple sentences or one complex sentence. Try to create one sentence out of the following sentences. Often, the first sentence can start with or contain an –ing verb. [Instuctors: You may wish to discuss the strengths and weaknesses of each potential rewrite. I suggest discussion should center on what information each rewrite emphasizes.]

Exercise G Continued:

1. The schoolboard attempted to block the addendum. The schoolboard voted without audience discussion. The schoolboard's choice angered some parents.

2. I remember my father wanted me to be an Olympic champion. I want to be an Olympic champion.

3.   I completed my dream. I became a teacher. I wanted to be a teacher my whole life.

4. I wanted to be a fireman my whole life. I became a fireman. I am proud of myself.

Once again, thinking mainly of nouns, verbs, and clauses, was there a pattern to your changes (nouns to verbs, verbs to nouns, clause to verb, etc.)?

Pronouns:

Pronouns are words that replace other nouns. We use them so often we do not even think about using them or how intricate the substitution process is. In speech, we have visual cues and tone of voice to help us make proper pronoun references. In writing, without these cues, readers may wonder which information the pronoun references. Here are some typical examples of correct everyday pronoun usage.

John broke the lawnmower and Bill fixed *it*.
These are the guilty men.
He and the astronauts are responsible for the astrophotography research.

Each of these sentences has a definite noun that is referenced. There is no confusion. However, even in the third example, the *he* who is the subject of the sentence does not appear in the sentence. It would appear in a paragraph similar to the following.

Bill Johnson is an astrophysicist and an amateur photographer. **He** *and the astronauts are responsible for the astrophotography research.*

Typically, people run into pronoun reference problems because of long sentences or multiple sentences. Your goal as a writer is to make certain your reader knows which previous noun the pronoun replaces. Typically, the rule for pronoun usage in formal writing stipulates that a pronoun references the last potential noun for which it could substitute. If this were always the case, the following sentences would not be confusing.

Alex drove Bill to the movies, and he said he had a good time.

The state of Alabama sued an offshore drilling company, and they lost.

He should reference Bill. *They* should reference the offshore drilling company. However, this would hardly be the assumption in everyday speech. Often, rewriting is the clearest option.

1a. Alex drove Bill to the movies, and Bill said he had a good time.

or

1b. Alex drove Bill to the movies, and Alex said he had a good time.

2a. The state of Alabama sued an offshore drilling company, and Alabama lost.

or

2b. The state of Alabama sued an offshore drilling company, and the company lost.

Pronouns are also used in everyday speech to start sentences. Often, these pronouns reference nothing in particular.

3a. *It* sure is a hot one today.

It in this sentence can technically be nothing other than the day. The sentence seems to be saying "The day sure is a hot one today." While this statement is normal, acceptable, and hardly noticeable in informal conversation, sentences of this type can typically be rewritten.

3b. Today sure is a hot one.

Here are several more formal examples:

4a. It is always easier to rewrite than to patch-up your sentences.

4b. *Rewriting is always easier than patching-up your sentences.*

5a. There was a reason the building closed.

5b. *The building was closed for a reason.*

The Cleft Sentence:

The cleft sentence allows focus to be shifted, much like other stylistic varieties. While sentence-starting pronouns such as "it" and "there" pepper our speech and writing, it is obvious they are not a necessity. The cleft sentence allows a writer to place focus on any of the various elements in the sentence.

A branch in the road caused the accident.
What caused the accident was a branch in the road.

Thick fog reduced the visibility to zero.
What reduced visibility to zero was the thick fog.

It was John that shingled the roof of Dave's house.
It was Dave's house that John shingled.
It was shingling that John put on Dave's house.

Notice how each of the three pieces of information can easily be shifted by starting with a pronoun. Starting a sentence with a pronoun, then, is much like the other subjects in this chapter. Pronoun use can both bolster or hinder writing. Your awareness of how you are using these tools in your writing will predict your level of success. If you choose a sentence pattern that delays information or creates a longer sentence structure, you should have a good reason for doing so.

Exercise H. Rewrite the following sentences as two other cleft sentences. Then rewrite the sentence to avoid the cleft sentence (*it, there, what,* etc.). There will be several possibilities.
What it was was a whistleblower that the senate gave protection.

1.

2.

3.

It is the college president that received the donation from alumni.

1.

2.

3.

Sentence Fragments:

You saw in earlier examples how clauses can contain only some of the parts needed to be a complete sentence. Fragments typically occur when punctuation is absent or misused. Fragments should typically be added on to the previous or following full sentence.

I used to sing alot. In the church choir.

The fountain of youth has never been found for many reasons. Including the impossibility of its existence.

Because of plentiful rain. After many years of drought. The Irish Potato Famine eventually ended.

Coffee should not be taken by children. Because their growth is stunted.

Fragments can be hard to spot when surrounded by full sentences that complete the thought, as in the above examples. They are easier to spot if you read "between the periods."

In the church choir.

Including the impossibility of its existence.

Because of plentiful rain.

After many years of drought.

Because their growth is stunted.

How do you recognize these as fragments? First, try your ear. If you still can't tell, look for a subject and verb (and maybe an object). Notice that many of these examples lack verbs. The last example lacks something else. What is it?

Exercise I: Fix the following fragments by either changing the punctuation to combine it with the surrounding sentence or by turning the fragment into its own sentence. Base your changes on clear and simple sentences.

1. New York, New York is big. Like Chicago.

2. He ran track. Back in high school.

3. Eliminating violence from the world will require many requirements. Such as brotherhood, discussion, and tolerance.

4. Canada's healthcare outranks that of the U.S. For example, cheap pills for seniors, cheap surgery for the ill, and inexpensive doctor's visits.

Fragments are dicey territory. Writing is loaded with them for stylistic effect. They tend to sound spoken, and fragments can convey emphasis because they purposely ignore the longer, formal sentence.

New York is big. Real Big.
I've got no money. Zero.
Lower prices. Today only.

As always, be aware of your fragments. Ask yourself if trading formality for stylistic effect is appropriate. Also ask yourself if the surrounding sentences clearly prepare your reader for fragmented information.

Run-Ons:

Run-on sentences are independent clauses that have not been punctuated properly. Typical fixes are with a comma and conjunction (and, or, nor, for, so, yet) or a semicolon.

The potatoes needed to be cooked at 200 degrees and the onion neededed to be kept raw.

becomes

The potatoes needed to be cooked at 200 degrees, and the onions needed to be kept raw.

or

The potatoes needed to be cooked at 200 degrees; the onions needed to be kept raw.

We will discuss punctuation to close the chapter. Please go to the punctuation section now if you are not familiar with commas or the semicolon.

Exercise J: Identify any run-on sentences, splices, or fragments and fix them appropriately.

1. The computer Deep Blue beat a chess champion but I can't remember his name.

2. You owe me thirteen quid or I'll smack you.

3. I like to think that, if it came down to it, I'd be heroic, I can't say I would be, though.

4. The military might often generates a military-industrial complex, Eisenhower warned against this situation.

5. If you're going to the store, buy me something nice and I'll pay you back.

6. Spilling oil into the sea is a regular occurrence for some oil refineries, but some people are pressing for stricter laws.

7. Officials acted quickly saving the school program for another year; helping children in need.

8. Because I wanted to oblige the city's public transportation program I've taken the train everyday this month; I will do the same next month.

Although we could go on forever, I'll stop this churning and turning of sentences, half-sentences, and bits of information here. You and your instructor can continue this process, gaining an awareness of the mobility of sentence parts along the way. You should certainly do this with your own sentences whenever they feel long or off the mark from the thought you wish to capture. I hope you see how clauses, fragments, half-sentences, nouns, and verbs can be shifted and combined for two purposes. The first purpose is always clarity of communication. The second purpose is style, which is also an integral part of communication.

Verbs:

Verbs assert that something occurred or exists. This means they can be *active*, as in a sentence like **John tossed the ball**, or it means they can portray a *state*, as in **I am hungry**, or simply **I am**.

"Be" Verbs:

Be verbs (is, are, was, were) are the most basic verbs in language. In English, they fall under a category known as *linking verbs*. Often seen as weak verbs because they lack action, image, and other "active" qualities that carry meaning, "be" verbs typically connect two ideas to each other. Because these verbs are the most common verbs in English, they often can't be avoided. Yet first drafts may contain "be" verbs that could be replaced by "action" verbs, which will be discussed momentarily.

Exercise K. Identify the "be" verbs in the following.
1. I am an adult.
2. The people down the street were really angry.
3. We are out of sorts.
4. The neighborhood watchmen were misunderstood.
5. Old pizza is not good.
6. Donald is on the roof.
7. Danny was in the driveway all day.
8. Science was absent during the Middle Ages.

As you can see, "be" verbs often function as something of an "equals" sign. These "be" verbs are hard to replace with action verbs. In addition to "be" verbs, there are many other verbs (get, had, have, etc.) that sometimes are required to bridge ideas in a sentence, yet these default verbs are often only our first choice and disguise better verb choices. Part of your rewriting process should pay strong attention to verb choice, always noting whether linking verbs are part of the tense (relation of an event to the present), whether linking verbs are portraying a state, as in the above examples, or whether the verbs are simply weak and could be rewritten with more "active" verbs.

Linking Verbs:

Linking verbs are a general term for important function verbs that also portray states. "Be" verbs are one example of a linking verb. Other examples of linking verbs are *seems*, *feels*, *looks*, *appears*, and *become*. While these linking verbs can be required verbs in some situations, these verbs can often disguise stronger active verbs. (If you can substitute a "be" verb and not change the sentence meaning, then you have a linking verb.)

Exercise L. Identify the linking verbs in the following sentences and choose stronger verbs to replace each.

1. Abraham Lincoln became a supporter of the Emancipation Proclamation during the middle of the Civil War.

2. The robin appeared on the branch.

3. The television show appears to be last night's winner.

4. The Marshall Plan seemed a building block of post-war European construction.

5. I felt a growing happiness all night long.

Verbs and Tense:

As mentioned, not all verbs that appear weak are actually weak verbs. Many verbs that carry no "meaning" that can be put into noun form can carry meaning relating to the time structure in a sentence. You may remember studying tenses such as past perfect, present perfect, past progressive, present progressive, and others during past English courses.

Exercise M: Read the following sentences and identify why the verbs are not simply weak verbs, but are important to the aspect of time the sentence communicates.

> I would have gone to the game, but no one asked.
> I have run every year since '98.
> When I retire, I will have saved 2 million dollars.
> I am playing basketball on Friday nights.
> I had had enough.
> I was speeding to the wedding.
> The clerk has been given help during this shift.
> The shopper should have had an easier time finding socks.
> The politician might have been called dishonest by his opponent.
> The kids have driven her crazy because they have been yelling for hours.

Each of the above sentences has multiple verbs that act as a unit and cannot be edited out without changing the sentence's sense of time or causation. The relationship of the past and present the speaker of each sentence wishes would be changed if these phrases were treated as "weak" verbs. Sentences with complex time relationships can be edited for clarity, but a good editor will always ask if they have changed the writer's intention when changing a verb phrase. Also, these lengthier verb phrases, often required to communicate past/present relationships, easily confuse a reader if not properly conjugated or not properly written to maintain the past/present relationships in surrounding sentences.

Action Verbs:

Now note the "action" verbs in the following sentences. These verbs convey a certain meaning rather than simply bridging the subject and predicate of the sentence. While some action verbs are metaphorical and personify objects, others are simply verbs containing ideas.

I spilled my coffee.
The people down the street rioted after the soccer match.
We launched a new campaign.
The neighborhood watchmen tackled the criminal.
Danny crippled the car's transmission.

Many action verbs can exist as nouns. *Be* verbs, you will notice, cannot be turned into nouns. Thus, action verbs contain "meaning" in the way that nouns do.

Verb: spilled
Noun:

Verb: rioted
Noun:

Verb: launched
Noun:

Verb: tackled
Noun:

Verb: crippled
Noun:

Because verbs and nouns contain the same meaning from a common root word, often times initial drafts will have weak verbs and strong nouns that can be shifted into strong verbs.

Exercise N. Change a noun in the following sentences into an active verb. Also notice what types of verbs are replaced in these sentences by active verbs.

1. The people down the street get angry easily.

2. The people down the street had a riot after the soccer match.

3. John is a maker of soap carvings.

4. Bob is the new program's implementer.

5. Come to a stop.

6. The truck is a delivery truck for a bread company.

7. Since the last baseball game, Ralph became a supporter of the Yankees.

8. Electing a new president is a requirement calling for voter awareness.

Selecting an active verb is not always as easy as changing a noun to a verb. Often times, choosing an active verb depends upon considering all the options for verbs that exist in your vocabulary. Thesauruses can be helpful as well. The following is an example of an active but plain verb disguising more specific active verbs.

The man *walked* across the street.

The man *shuffled* across the street.
The man *ambled* across the street.
The man *sped* across the street.
The man *raced* across the street.
The man *trudged* across the street.

Walked is an active verb, but you can see how different active verbs enhance a particular meaning a writer or speaker desires. You can also consider a previous example using the linking verb *appears*.

The robin *appeared* on the branch.

The robin *glided* onto the branch.
The robin *floated* onto the branch.
The robin *landed* on the branch.
The robin *weighted* down the branch.
The robin *nested* on the branch.

Now you can see that the linking verb *appeared* may not always be the strongest choice. If it can mean all of these things, then the verb is not specific to the exact meaning the writer desires. *Glided* and *floated* are specific to how the robin approached the branch and "appeared" on the branch. *Landed* and *weighted* do not explain the robin's approach; rather, they explain the robin's position post-flight, and *weighted* describes the robin's physical effect on the branch. *Nested* is similar to *landed* and *weighted*, but it is a long-term event. While the first four choices all seem to describe the immediate appearance of the robin, the fifth describes a long-term event. Thus, in these five sentences we have three different types of context. Each would be dependent upon the overall paragraph's purpose describing the approach, the physical effect, or the long-term event. The linking verb *appeared* captured none of these. Active verbs will allow you to execute your writing goals with precision.

Most academic writing will not deal with men walking or robins appearing. Here is an example closer to academic and professional writing.

The superior court changed the law concerning campaign financial contributions.

The verb *changed* is active—the "change" actively affected a law. However, much like the *walked* example, we don't get the exact change. The writer would then have to explain the change in the following sentence. Why not mention the type of change specifically if possible?

The superior court abolished the law concerning campaign financial contributions.
The superior court refined the law concerning campaign financial contributions.

While each of these sentences require more explanation simply because this "change" requires lengthy explanation, each of these sentences signals the reader toward a more specific type of "change" that will be detailed in upcoming paragraphs.

Here is another example of a sentence with nondescript verb phrase. While this verb phrase is functional, find verbs that narrow the direction of the change. Notice how thinking of this sentence in simple subject/verb/object terms has *opened up* the possibility of stronger verbs. The initial phrase, "said no," actually robs a writer of vocabulary. An awareness of basic language and information structures (subject/verb/object) allow you to see the sentence in all its possibilities.

The woman *said no* to her accuser.

The woman _____ her accuser.

Example: rebuffed

"Reporting" Verbs:

All this talk of verbs leads us to one final category important to formal academic and professional writing: reporting verbs. Reporting verbs are verbs that are common to writing that take the ideas of others and uses it to forward its own ideas. Because academic and professional writing are always building a base of ideas upon which the thesis depends, reporting verbs are a good category of verbs to master. While there are many "reporting" verbs and some are more specific to certain fields, here is a short list of verbs that can be used to "report."

reported	suggested	denied	validated
stated	purported	negated	indicated
reminded	delineated	argued	discussed
described	told	disputed	disproved
assumed	asked	conceded	noted
illustrated	promised	investigated	predicted
demonstrated	explained	evaluated	testified
recognized	predicated	analyzed	communicated
compared	observed	indicated	
concluded	verified	criticized	

Some of these reporting verbs pepper our everyday speech, and some are more formal and may require repeated use before they become natural to your writing and speech. Each carries with it the danger of misuse you saw in the previous examples. Also, remember each of these verbs carries with it a certain meaning. "Purports" has a much different meaning than "delineates." You must be familiar with how to use each so as to use it discriminately in your own ideas without distorting the original idea. Ideally, you should be able to rearrange these verbs according to the degree of certainty each suggests.

Exercise O: Search through the verbs in the following sentences and passages. Replace any weak verbs with stronger verbs, and use reporting verbs where appropriate.

1. It is said that 1.5 million African hospital beds contain AIDS patients. Research shows that this number will continue to grow without international intervention. Multiple international organizations have said that an emphasis on condom distribution as a deterrent has not met earlier projections.

2. The oil boom that Louisiana went through after the start of World War II reached its peak in 1969. The proposed review will talk about why the oil industry is the major reason why Lafayette developed into a large and successful city.

3. Because of the emphasis on Marxism, some humanities scholars have turned toward older forms of secular humanism. This is seen in the work of Harold Bloom. Bloom's work shows a combination of historical information and close reading. Biographical material can also be used or not used.

For the fourth example, find the strong verbs, especially the reporting verbs, and change them to weaker verbs that complete the sentence but lack specificity and conviction.

4. Meteorologists have documented accurate climate changes in the United States for most of the Twentieth Century. While conservative reports promise slowly rising sea waters, less conservative reports predict many coastal areas will be threatened by ocean waters within the next several decades. While the United States Government has been slow to explain these findings to the public, the international scientific community publicly communicates this information on a daily basis.

Now, rewrite again, replacing your weaker verbs with a new reporting verbs that are accurate to the original reporting verbs' meanings.

Transitive and Intransitive Verbs:

Some verbs require an *object* that finishes the idea implied by the verb. Other verbs seem to stand on their own. Those verbs that can stand on their own are intransitive. Those that cannot are transitive. While the study of transitive and intransitive verbs is not an issue of writing, but one of grammar, noting the difference between these two verb qualities can help you make sense of your own or a colleague's imperfect writing.

First, let's look at several examples of correct transitive and intransitive verbs.

Intransitive:

I jumped.
The senate voted.
Although I tried, I failed.

Transitive:

I own ten paintbrushes.
When I was young, I collected butterflies.
The astronauts will fix the satellite during their space walk.

Intransitive verbs are finite actions requiring no information after them to complete the idea. The transitive sentences are types of meaning that require more information. Leaving out their objects proves this true.

I own.
When I was young, I collected.
The astronauts will fix.

Each sentence leaves one asking what one owns, collected, or will fix. The most practical application of the transitive/intransitive distinction and of verb use in general to writing stems from mistakes common during a writer's growth process—misused vocabulary.

I internalized during the night.
New York's Museum of Modern Art exhibited brilliantly and continues to do so.
Shaw transcended during his middle period.

The question for each of these sentences is "what"? What is internalized? What is exhibited? What did Shaw transcend? Each of these verbs requires an object, even if a reader can figure out what was internalized or exhibited from previous information in the paragraph. The easiest way to fix awkward sentences like those above is to consult a dictionary to check out what type of verb you are using. This is especially important when using verbs you have not used much in writing. As you progress in your chosen major, the vocabulary you develop will be new and highly specific. As you grow into ownership of a more formal vocabulary, you may often have to consult a dictionary or thesaurus.

Rewrite each of the following sentences. Provide a noun object for each of the verbs requiring a "what." Not all of the sentences require editing. A variety of answers are possible, so answers are not included. Answers should be discussed as a class.

1. The Nielson ratings collect weekly.

2. Each member of the platoon fulfilled his duties responsibly.

3. He and the other members solidified.

4. While Martin Luther King, Jr. received, Malcolm X militantly agitated for rights.

5. The architecture of I.M. Pei stuns and impresses.

6. Whether on or off the court, Michael Jordan is a leader who inhibits and exudes.

As writers progress, they may exhibit another peculiarity based in vocabulary development that can relate to the transitive/intransitive distinction. This peculiarity is when a writer uses nouns as verbs. In the first example, a transitive verb is needed. The second example is simply a noun misused as a verb.

The bank assetted Rockefeller one million in equity.
The mayoral decision was to terminalize the project.

A quick check of the dictionary would have suggested that "asset" is a noun that cannot be made into a verbal. "Credited" may be a better choice. "Terminalize" is not a word; however, "terminate" is a verb that would work well, although the writer has included a potentially unnecessary "be" verb as well. Each of these verbs stem from the noun "terminate." Correctness depends upon a trip to the dictionary to ensure you've made the right choice. Yet I do not want to give you the idea that the English language is extremely rigid and unchanging. A word such as "assetted" may be used in some banking or financial circles that most people are not a part of. And recently in popular culture the verb *conversate* appeared, although we already had the verb *converse* doing the same work. Language is a complex system that is always changing according to how people are speaking and writing. Conventions and usage will change as the new becomes old.

One more type of mistake is common as people move into more formal academic and professional writing. Using awkward or odd prepositions to make incongruent sentence parts fit.
He demands listeners to take action.

Due to past experience, the legal profession has <u>accredited toward</u> teaching lawyers more business skill to better understand their future employers.

Dr. Hofstader <u>emphasized upon</u> an increase in vice taxes to provide for education revenue.

In the first example, the sentence should read
He demands that listeners take action.
He commands listeners to take action.

While each change is a small distinction, your readers and colleagues will either know or "feel" that something is wrong with your word choice. Small mistakes like this can undermine your credibility with your reader. While the explanation as to why *demands* is not correct in the above sentence is a lengthy explanation requiring intricate knowledge of grammar, the easiest way to erase mistakes when working with formal language is simply to read as much as possible. Exposure to correct usage of typical verbs in longer and formal sentences is a much better way to improve your writing than learning the dozens of abstract grammatical rules for which there are ∴ as many exceptions as rules. Reading will help improve your vocabulary, your sentence structure, your organizational skills, and your communication abilities without ever picking up a pen or sitting at a keyboard.

Often times we cannot find the word we are looking for and grab whatever word is available, using our language knowledge to make it fit. These mistakes are part of the development of a writer, but if you are ever to naturally choose the correct word, you will need to consult a dictionary to see if your chosen word is actually a functional verb! Also, remember that you will often already have a word in your vocabulary that is specific and correct, so be careful in choosing elevated vocabulary. You risk overwriting and missing a chance to communicate your ideas as clearly as possible.

Active and Passive Voice:

Active and passive voice depend upon the arrangement of ideas in a sentence. If the subject/actor of the sentence acts upon the object, then the sentence is active. If the subject/actor receives the action in the verb phrase, then the sentence is passive. If you prefer, you can think of the subject/actor as a "doer" or "performer of the action" as well. However, not all sentences have actors included, and actors do not always need to be human or animate (Examples: the wind, gravity, fate, etc.).

For example, **The dog bit the mailman** is in active voice. We see the dog doing the biting. The sentence components put the actor of the actions first. In **The mailman was bitten by the dog** we do not have an emphasis on the dog acting. Rather, the emphasis is on the object that received the action.

Exercise P. First, identify the subject/actor in the sentence. Next, identify the object/receiver of the action. Then identify whether the following are in active or passive voice.

1. The boy smashed the vase.

2. String Theory rewrote the laws of physics.

3. I spent too much money.

4. The treaty was rescinded by the British government.

5. British Columbia broke the promise.

Although there is no way to predict when to use active or passive sentences, active sentences are preferred in most genres of writing. (Science writing can be an exception.) Typically, situations where a writer wishes to emphasize the object and not the doer are the situations using passive voice. This will be discussed more in later sections dealing with paragraphing—how and when a writer chooses active or passive voice always depends upon the entire paragraph's discussion of the subject/actor, action, and object.

Notice that passive voice sentences all contain one unique characteristic. Instead of a single verb, they must have a "be" verb along with their main verb. This is one easy way to identify passive voice sentences. Often times, passive voice will include the preposition "by" to include the actor in the sentence.

The vase was smashed by the boy.
A mile was run by me in my green socks.
Too much money was spent by me.
The British government rescinded the treaty.
The promise was broken by British Columbia.

However, not every sentence includes the "doer" of the action, yet the sentence is complete. Even without a "doer," the sentence is still passive.

We were arrested.
Phil and Marcy were married.

We were arrested. (by the police)
Phil and Marcy were married. (by their priest)

Exercise Q. Identify each of the following sentences as active or passive. Rewrite each in the opposite voice. As always, imagine what writing situations would call for each sentence being written in the active or the passive voice.

1. He was seen by your parents last night.

2. They were being audited by the securities commission for over eight months.

3. We might have been evaluated during the interview by the manager.

4. Victims of the earthquake were sent relief.

5. He was considered an outstanding player by the coaches.

6. This year, the orphans should have been helped by the social welfare agency.

7. We were being assisted by our instructor for two hours in the classroom.

8. The car was being tuned up by the very knowledgeable mechanic.

9. I accidentally called the mechanic a greasemonkey.

10. The mechanic laughed at my car.

11. The two parties carefully designed next year's education program.

12. He has been taught Spanish for three years by her.

You have probably noticed that writing in active voice creates less wordier sentences. In complex sentences, active voice can create much clearer sentences.

Many students in the school tasted Thursday's meatloaf in Friday's lunch, but **it was eaten by them** anyway. (passive)

Many students in the school tasted Thursday's meatloaf in Friday's lunch, but **they ate it** anyway. (active)

"The Big Picture": Active and Passive Voice in a Paragraph

Identify which sentences in the following paragraph are passive sentences. Does the passive voice seem appropriate in these situations? Ask yourself why the passive voice seems appropriate in these situations.

The American worker combines dedication with innovation (1). Statistics prove this true (2). Ninety percent of American workers claim their job as a component of self-esteem(3). Sixty percent reveal they would miss their job(4). Each of these dedicated men and women devise a means to balance work and play in their busy lives(5). Yet the middle and working classes of Americans were robbed of wage increases equal to inflation as early as the 1970s(6). By the 1980s, stagflation wreaked havoc upon the economy(7). Americans were made to work harder just to break even.(8)

Jobs disappeared overseas(9). Many blue-collar towns lost their major sources of employment(10). These sources of employment were not replaced by the government or industry(11).....

Answer to "The Big Picture":

Sentences 6 and 8 are passive. I would suggest that in this passage, we see the first reason for passive sentences: people being acted upon by an unnamed force. In this case, the American worker is being acted upon by the economic forces, not a particular person. The American worker is a victim without a particular oppressor. Much like the example *They were married (by the priest)*, sentences 6 and 8 are simply missing the "by" that would mention an actor/doer. A writer could easily provide an actor/doer for these sentences:

6. *Yet the middle and working classes of Americans were robbed of wage increases equal to inflation **by bad economic policy** as early as the 1970s.*

8. *Americans were made to work harder **by economic necessity** just to break even.*

Often these "invisible forces" are implied or could simply be too many "doers" to name. So they are left out and the reader simply realizes the "doer" will appear at some point in the argument. The beginning sentences are active because the "doer" is the American worker. The "doer" in sentence 7 is "stagflation." Although this a switch from the American worker as "doer," this change makes sense. "Stagflation" is part of the unnamed "doer" that victimizes American workers in sentences 6 and 8. Thus, sentences 6, 7, and 8 seem to be a new idea separate from the first five sentences championing the American worker.

In paragraph two, sentence 11, we see the other major reason for passive voice. Whenever a writer wishes to continue discussing a subject in a new sentence without any information in between, the passive voice provides an outlet to do so. Sentence 10 ends with *major sources of employment*, and sentence 11 begins with *These sources of employment*. Thus, passive voice seems a good choice. Although this breaks both the "write in active voice" rule, as well as the "combine like information" rule, the paragraph may be more successful because it breaks these rules.

Remember that it is impossible to predict whether a sentence should be active or passive without knowing what information came before your sentence and what information will come after your sentence. Equally important is the genre of writing. Each of these criteria should be applied when you are checking your drafts for voice. Later sections dealing with paragraphing will discuss these choices in excerpts from student essays.

Sentence Types:

The four sentence types:

Interrogative
Imperative
Declarative
Exclamatory

Declarative sentences are statements about the world that are not questions, commands, demands, suggestions, or exclamations. Most sentences are declarative sentences. I suppose you could say that declarative sentences lack character. After all, imperative sentences and interrogative sentences require the interplay of two people, speaker and listener. Exclamatory sentences are all in rush and excited, which most people would do in front of at least a one-person audience. Declarative sentences are simply informational, stating something about the world that may not depend upon the actions, opinions, or answers of the speaker or audience. However, this is also their greatest strength. Here are some basic declarative sentences.

I stopped in a small town.
Harold is a fireman.
The quick brown fox jumped over the lazy hens.
IPOD sales are a direct threat to the music industry's sales and profits.
Structural anthropology examines similar societal patterns practiced in multiple societies.
Clarence Thomas is the most conservative African-American justice to reside in the Supreme Court.

Your earliest memories are probably of being drilled on the four sentence types. Beyond identifying them, use this knowledge to help you communicate and argue effectively. Because exposition and argument depend on statements and propositions taken to be truthful or based in sound reason, writers typically choose declarative sentences when expressing their opinions and explaining themselves. Declarative sentences also carry the added advantage of seeming objective and not based as much in the emotions of the writer. Imperative sentences can seem bossy. Exclamatory sentences can make a writer's voice or a writer's idea seem based more in emotion or excitement than sound reasoning. For these reasons, imperatives and exclamatories are not used as frequently as declarative sentences. Consider the following sentences. One sounds professional and carries the gravity of formal writing. The other sounds spoken and informal.

The American Paleontology Society overturned a previous ruling on the age of the Wooly Mammoth.

The American Paleontology Society overturned a previous ruling on the age of the Wooly Mammoth!

As you try to build authority and trust with your audience, small decisions such as sentence type can have large ripple effects on your level of formality. Also, punctuation and sentence type can determine if you are perceived as balanced, well-spoken, and ethical, or if you are excitable and prone to rushing to judgment.

Here is a pair of sentences exemplifying the reductive quality of the exclamatory sentence:

The current military action in the Middle East is nothing more than blood for oil.

No Blood for Oil!

While these examples are a similar idea written differently, you can see how the exclamation point can carry with it the connotation of extreme emotion. Your reader may see the second, even if you've written something akin to the first with the addition of an exclamation point. You can imagine the first being a basic thesis statement for a balanced argumentative essay. Sound reasoning and claims could easily follow this statement. The second example seems both too explosive and too inarticulate to function as even a basic thesis statement because it may alienate those it wishes to persuade immediately.

A similar quality of unbalanced emotion can exist in the imperative sentence, but this isn't necessarily true. Here are some everyday examples:

Be careful.
Run away.
Stop it.
Change your ways.
Know thyself.

Now consider the following uses of the imperative in a writing context:

Give up your right to bear arms immediately.

Surrendering the individual's right to gun ownership would decrease gun deaths in the United States by thousands every year.

The second again seems much more balanced. If you've read closely, you'll notice the second, more balanced example does include cause/effect information the first example does not include. This may be because declarative sentences lend themselves to a strong thesis statement and reasoning simply through their style. However, this may not always be true. Still, consider the following:

Give up your right to bear arms immediately and decrease gun deaths in the United States by thousands every year.

Even with the same cause/effect information, this last example still lends the statement a "pushiness" that most readers will notice. Because we have been exposed to so many essays and arguments starting like the first, it is questionable whether or not good cause and effect reasoning at the sentence's end can overcome the unusual imperative start of this purported essay. I would suggest that the imperative in each of these examples feels more like a slogan

The Comma:

Commas are used for a variety of reasons. They may separate nouns, verbs, and clauses. If you have already worked through this chapter, then you have been exposed to most of the following comma uses.

1. Commas separate items in a series (parallelism). Whether or not the final comma before the conjunction is needed depends upon what editorial style you are using. Please check an appropriate handbook for an answer. I have chosen to include the comma, but this needn't be so.

    The burglars stole my bike, my wallet, and my new grill.

    To be, to have, and to succeed are all admirable goals.

2. Commas separate parallel adjectives without conjunctions or not in a list.

    When I bought my car, it was a cool, bad street racer. Now it is a junky, funky rustbucket.

3. Commas are used with introductory phrases in a sentence. Introductory phrases are always dependent clauses requiring a complete sentence afterward.

    Although he ran the race well, he lost by several steps.

    Far from the earth, the moon comes out to greet the night.

4. Commas should separate modifying clauses.

    With Dave's homework around him, Chuck tried to finish his assignment.

    Tragically, he didn't see the sword was dipped with poison.

    Sometimes short introductory clauses omit the comma.

    From now on I'll walk.

5. Commas are used to divide independent clauses (complete sentences) from each other to avoid run-ons.

    The magazine was started in 1942, and it had doubled in size by 1948.

    She couldn't get angry, nor could she get even.

6. Commas should not be used in what is known as a restrictive phrase, but they should be used in a non-restrictive phrase.

    Restrictive phrases offer information that modifies a noun in the sentence. It is not extra information.

    *The streetcleaners need wages **that are livable**.*

    Livable directly modifies *wages*. If you remove *livable* from the sentence, we don't know that streetcleaners are paid at all! That is not what the sentence intends to communicate. *Livable* is not extra information.

Non-restrictive:

    *The streetcleaners need new uniforms, **which are blue**.*

The color of the uniforms has nothing to do with why they are needed. Thus, the information is extra and is separated from the kernel sentence with a comma.

1) My girlfriend Becky who lives in Minneapolis is also my best friend.

2) My girlfriend Becky, who lives in Minneapolis, is also my best friend.

In the first example, the speaker has more than one girlfriend named Becky—*who lives in Minneapolis* is required information to differentiate her another girlfriend named Becky living in a different city. In the second non-restrictive example, the city she lives in is extra information. The commas serve to remove it from the kernel sentence *My girlfriend is my best friend.* When a clause of this type adds extra information to part of the kernel sentence, the clause is known as an appositive clause.

7. Commas also set off parenthetical expressions, which are similar to appositive clauses. Parenthetical expressions add extra information as well. Sometimes they add speaker opinion. Other times they modify.

    The thirty-five hour work week, it is said, will never find a home in America.

    I picked up after last night's party, more or less.

8. Commas separate contrasting information.

    I need a 93% on this exam, not an 85%.

    He chased his dream, but never caught it.

    Unlike his father, he became a banker.

9. Commas should be used to separate your own words and a direct quotation.

    "Ask not what your country can do for you, but what you can do for your country," stated John F. Kennedy.

    John F. Kennedy stated, "Ask not what your country can do for you, but what you can do for your country."

    However, do not use a comma if you blend your words with the quotation to make a single sentence.

    Benjamin Franklin said that "A penny saved is a penny earned."

    Elvis sang that he was "down on the end of lonely street."

10. Commas should separate the day and year, as well as the year and subsequent information.
    Franklin Roosevelt solemnly proclaimed that December 7, 1941, is a day that will live in infamy.

    Commas are not required if the date is inverted or if only the month and year appear.
    On 7 December 1941 Pearl Harbor was attacked.

    December 1941 Pearl Harbor was attacked.

    Finally, commas can also be used anytime information is confusing.
    That that will be will be

    Interestingly, the findings report that those of the legal age that could should.

    become
    That that will be, will be.

    Interestingly, the findings report that those of the legal age that could, should.

The Semicolon:

The semicolon requires an independent clause (a complete sentence) on each side of it. It is used to show a finer or stronger relationship between two sentences than a period would.

Tolerance is noble; forgiveness is divine.

I am returning to my hometown; I will never leave.

Often, a conjunctive adverb (however, thus, moreover, therefore, otherwise, nevertheless, etc.) appears before the second sentence; thus, we see that the sentences are paired by a type of cause/effect relationship. The semicolon marks this.

Tolerance is noble; however, forgiveness is divine.

I am returning to my hometown; moreover, I will never leave.

The semicolon plus a conjunctive adverb emphasizes the speaker's heightened "attitude" toward the topic. We get a weighty attitude about forgiveness and the speaker's hometown in the above examples.

The Colon:

The colon has two basic functions. The first is to introduce a list.

To be a lawyer, one must do the following things: major in pre-law, perform well on standardized tests, and specialize once in law school.

Often, writers misuse the colon in the following way:

Camping requires items such as: a tent, a grill, insect repellent, and firewood.

Such as serves the same function as the colon—to introduce. Both are not required. Furthermore, neither may be required.

Camping requires items such as a tent, a grill, insect repellent, and firewood.

Camping requires the following items: a tent, a grill, insect repellent, and firewood.

Camping requires a tent, a grill, insect repellent, and firewood.

The second use of a colon is to introduce a definition.

Humankind suffers from one great flaw: humanness.

While he walked down the mountain, his feet felt only one sensation: the cold, dull thump of frostbite.

I learned something about myself that day: I am often afraid when I don't need to be.

Late-stage capitalism can be defined as only two things: opportunism and irresponsible growth.

Opportunism and irresponsible growth can be summed up in one idea: Late-stage capitalism.

Notice that each of these "definitions" is not a dictionary definition. Sometimes it is easier to think of these as two perfectly balanced statements rather than an old-fashioned dictionary definition. As mentioned early in this textbook, dictionary definitions often fail to capture large meaning, multiple meanings, and contextual meaning. The colon can help you glue a sentence-length defining idea to a sentence requiring explanation.

The colon has other functions as well, such as separating a greeting from the body of a letter. It it useful to remember that colon usage does not require complete sentences; semicolon usage does.

The Hyphen:

The hyphen serves many of the functions listed above for commas, semicolons, and colons. It can attach fragments to sentences, separate whole sentences, set off lists, and set off appositive information as well. Which type of punctuation the writer selects depends upon style, subject, and emphasis.

I used to run a lot—in high school.

The election of 1984 was one of the most predictable in history—except in Minnesota.

I really wish I had switched my major last year—I would be graduating in three semesters.

John's cousin—who lives in Cambodia—won't be back for two years.

Exercise S:

Rewrite the following sentences using appropriate punctutation. Some sentences may have several potential answers.

1. Should the president pass away the vice-president assumes the presidency.

2. I am investigating three things the limits of chemistry in botany the effects of mercury on saplings and any research that overlaps these subjects.

3. Talent is not natural, it is earned in private and displayed in public.

4. Consequently the army is becoming a necessary choice for young men and women no matter how much they wish to enroll in college immediately.

5. They serve with honor; pride; and humility.

6. I used to sing a lot. In the church choir.

7. The fountain of youth has never been found for many reasons. Including the impossibility of its existence.

8. Because of plentiful rain. After many years of drought. The Irish Potato Famine eventually ended.

9. Coffee should not be taken by children. Because their growth is stunted.

Closing:

Some errors make communication itself difficult. Other errors may be grammatically correct, but they hurt your ability to persuade your readers that your argument is a good one. Remember that the easiest way to master writing is simply to read as much as possible. All of these ideas are standard fare in our highly literate society, and the communications of your field will provide you with the professional vocabulary and style that allows you to communicate efficiently. Also, you should always remember that, despite all of these suggestions, your writing is first and foremost a *creative* activity. You will always have to make choices. The point of this chapter was not to give you hard and fast rules that guarantee your success as a writer. My goal in this chapter was to give you an awareness of likely difficulties as you transition toward a career based in writing, and I wanted you to have a criteria to begin to judge the potential success of your writing on the word level and sentence level.

Answers to Exercises:

Exercise A:

1. governor, California, time
2. hours, I (pronoun), town
3. I (pronoun), meals, evening
4. springtime, time
5. Johnny, town, weekend
6. Wisconsin, United States, 1848
7. Blink Theory, advertisements, quantity, exposure, quality, exposure
8. Experts, identity, part, images, society

Exercise B:

1. In terms of reciprocity, Chinese environmental policy is a tragedy played out in the weather patterns of neighboring countries.
2. Baseball's steroid policy contramands values of America today and baseball's past.
3. While the Marshall Plan did not cure Europe immediately, Europe's comeback took only several decades.

4. Initial investigations suggested that the senator was guilty of embezzlement for the misappropriation of funds.

5. Half time employees protested for adequate health care consisting of dental care and fair deductibles.

6. The scientific community declared that many minerals found on earth are found in the rest of the galaxy and predate earth's formation.

   The scientific community declared that many minerals found on earth predate earth's formation and are found in the rest of the galaxy.

7. Television and radio changed American society forever.

8. The helicopter and the M-16 were first used as weapons in the Vietnam War.

9. The jury debated for two hours. They voted three times before reaching a verdict.

   The jury debated for two hours and voted three times before reaching a verdict.

Exercise C:

1. Mercantilism has often existed in societies that traded internationally.

2. High school sports foster responsibility and build self-esteem.

3. Teens are often influenced to use steroids for better performance because their professional role models use them.

4. People are addicted to oil, and we must investigate alternative fuel sources.

5. Agricultural growth cannot sustain population growth.

6. Energy efficient light bulbs and unplugged appliances will make us use "green" priorities.

Exercise D:

1. Acknowledging my learning disability guaranteed me the help I needed for college success.

2. Choosing marketing provided me quality time and a livable salary.

3. Melting ice caps will present a danger to coastal cities within twenty years.

4. Whoever commits a crime should be punished.

Exercise E:

[Other editorial possibilities exist than those I've listed.]

1. The Brooks' commission's inconsistencies were found unforgivable by the public.

   The public found the Brooks' commission's inconsistencies unforgivable.

2. Non-curvilinear buildings are eyesores.

3. To investigate late-nineteenth-century crime, I used Sherlock Holmes' methodology.

4. The KGB agent's assassinations were classified within the Russian archives that also recorded trips to China and Cuba during the late 1940s.

5. The agency then offered one million dollars to compensate for illegal activities.

6. Pundits forecasted the economics for each month of the next two years.

    Pundits forecasted the month to month economics of the next two years.

Exercise F:

1. While Jerry told his boss he quit, his girlfriend waited in the car.

2. After he relented to the pressure to step down from office, the dictator resigned from his lifelong post.

3. Announcing their fundraiser, the clergy held a carwash and a booksale.

4   His face turning red, he called an ambulance and waited to be taken to the hospital.

5. While his girlfriend waited in the car, Jerry told his boss he quit.

6. Resigning from his lifelong post, the dictator relented to pressure to step down from office.

7. Later holding their car wash and book sale, the clergy announced their fundraiser.

8. Before he called an ambulance and waited to be taken to the hospital, he turned red in the face.

    ****It is questionable whether 5–8 are strong sentences when reversed. Sentence 5 may shift the emphasis from Jerry to his girlfriend. Sentences 6–8 may change the sense of time and causation implicit in the original sentences.*

Exercise G:

a) Trying to break the record

b) the man ran a mile

c) but failed to do so in under four minutes

1. [The schoolboard attempted to block the addendum.

    The schoolboard voted without audience discussion.

    The schoolboard's choice angered some parents.]

    Attempting to block the addendum, the schoolboard voted without audience discussion, angering some parents.

    Angering some parents, the schoolboard voted without audience discussion in an attempt to block the addendum.

2. [I remember my father wanted me to be an Olympic champion..

    I want to be an Olympic champion.]

    To honor my father's wishes, I want to be an Olympic champion.

3. [I completed my dream.

    I became a teacher.

    I wanted to be a teacher my whole life.]

    Wanting to be a teacher my whole life, I completed my dream and became a teacher.

[It is questionable whether the third component is needed. Including wanting and dreaming may be redundant.]

Completing my dream, I became a teacher.

4. [I wanted to be a fireman my whole life.

   I became a fireman.

   I am proud of myself.]

   After wanting to be a fireman my whole life, I proudly became one.

Exercise H:

1. What it was was the senate that gave the whistleblower protection.

2. What it was was protection that the senate gave the whistleblower.

3. The senate gave the whistleblower protection.

4. It is a donation that the college president received from the alumni.

5. It is the alumni that gave the college president a donation.

   or

   It is the alumni that gave a donation to the college president.

6. The college president received a donation from the alumni.

Exercise I:

1. New York is big—like Chicago.

   New York is big. Chicago is big also.

2. He ran track back in high school.

   Back in high school, he ran track.

3. Eliminating violence from the world will require brotherhood, discussion, and tolerance.

4. Canada's healthcare outranks U.S. healthcare. For example, Canadian healthcare provides cheap pills for seniors, cheap surgery for the ill, and inexpensive doctor's visits.

Exercise J:

1. The computer Deep Blue beat a chess champion, but I can't remember his name.

2. You owe me thirteen quid, or I'll smack you.

3. I like to think that if it came down to it I'd be heroic. I can't say I would be, though.

   A better rewording exists. A period or semicolon can still both be used.

   I like to think that if heroism was required, I'd be heroic; I can't say I would be, though.

4. The military might often generates a military-industrial complex. Eisenhower warned against this situation.

   The military might often generates a military-industrial complex; Eisenhower warned against this situation.

5. If you're going to the store, buy me something nice, and I'll pay you back.

6. Spilling oil into the sea is a regular occurrence for some oil refineries, but some people are pressing for stricter laws. (No error.)

7. Officials acted quickly, saving the school program for another year and helping children in need.

8. Because I wanted to oblige the city's public transportation program, I've taken the train everyday this month; I will do the same next month.

Exercise K:

1. am
2. were
3. are
4. were
5. is
6. is
7. was
8. was

Exercise L:

1. became
   Abraham Lincoln supported the Emancipation Proclamation during the middle of the Civil War.

2. appeared
(see later examples)

3. appears
   The television show won last night.

4. seemed
   The Marshall Plan founded post-war European construction.

5. felt
   My happiness grew all night long.

Exercise M:

Each verb pertains to the *tense*, the time of the event in relation to the time the sentence is spoken. Instructors should lead a class discussion as to why and how these verb phrases can be modified only the time and duration of the event do not change in a rewrite.

Exercise N:

1. The people down the street anger easily.
2. The people down the street rioted after the soccer match.

3. John makes soap carving.

4. Bob implemented the new program.

5. Stop.

6. The truck delivers for a bread company.

7. Since the last baseball game, Ralph supports the Yankees.

8. Electing a new president requires voter awareness.

Exercise O: (Reporting verbs are in **bold**. Other changes are in *italics*. The substitute verbs I have chosen may not be your own.)

1. It is **reported** that 1.5 million African hospital beds contain AIDS patients. Research **illustrates** that this number will continue to grow without international intervention. Multiple international organizations **conclude** that an emphasis on condom distribution as a deterrent has not met earlier projections.

2. *Louisiana's post World War II oil boom* reached its peak in 1969. My review will *explain* how the oil industry *contributed to* Lafayette's development into a large and successful city.

3. Because of the emphasis on Marxism, some humanities scholars have turned toward older forms of secular humanism. This is **demonstrated** in the work of Harold Bloom. Bloom's work *includes* a combination of historical information and close reading. Bloom may also *utilize* biographical material.

[For the fourth example, you were to find strong verbs, especially reporting verbs, and change them to weaker verbs that complete the sentence but lack specificity and conviction.]

4. Meteorologists have *had* accurate climate changes in the United States for most of the Twentieth Century. While conservative reports **show** slowly rising sea waters, less conservative reports **show** many coastal areas will be threatened by ocean waters within the next several decades. While the United States Government has been slow to **tell** these findings to the public, the international scientific community publicly **says** this information on a daily basis.

[For the second part, you were to choose new reporting verbs.]

4. Meteorologists have **recorded** accurate climate changes in the United States for most of the Twentieth Century. While conservative reports **indicate** slowly rising sea waters, less conservative reports **promise** many coastal areas will be threatened by ocean waters within the next several decades. While the United States Government has been slow to **introduce** these findings to the public, the international scientific community publically **verifies** this information on a daily basis.

Exercise P:

1. boy, vase: active

2. String Theory, laws: active

3. I, money: active

4. British government, treaty: passive

5. British Columbia, promise: active

Exercise Q:

1. *passive*:   Active version: Your parents saw him last night.

2. *passive*:   Active version: The securities commission audited them for over eight months.

3. *passive*:   Active version: The manager might have evaluated us during the interview.

4. *active*:   Passive version: Relief was sent to the victims of the hurricane.

5. *passive*:   Active version: The coaches considered him an outstanding player.

6. *passive*:   Active version: The social welfare agency should have helped the orphans this year.

7. *passive*:   Active version: Our instructor assisted us for two hours in the classroom.

8. *passive*:   Active version: The very knowledgeable mechanic tuned up the car.

9. *active*:   Passive version: The mechanic was accidentally called a greasemonkey by me.

10. *active*:   Passive version: My car was laughed at by the mechanic.

11. *active*:   Passive version: Next year's education program was carefully designed by the two parties.

12. *passive*:   Active version: She has taught him Spanish for three years.

Exercise R:

1. The expectations were to be good, to run with the best, and to go until the finish.

   The expectations were to be good, run with the best, and go until the finish.

2. The results were to be steadfast, to be resolved, and to be sensible.

   The results were to be steadfast, resolved, and sensible.

3. Experts predict that a major quake will hit the coast again, causing an upsurge in coastal erosion and salinizing the coastal farmland.

4. *There is nothing technically wrong with this example.*

   His former illnesses include pneumonia, asthma, and a cold.

5. *This example should have either two modifiers and prepositional phrases, or two nouns.*

   In this age, actors have to be gorgeous in looks and great in their acting.

   In this age, actors have to be a gorgeous person and a great actor.

6. Stan can fix a car like no other and can fix a television too.

   Stan is someone who can fix a car like no other and who can fix a television too.

7. *Surged works as a verb for highs and lows, but a second verb is needed for "balance." This second verb should be in the same tense as surged.*

   The Dow surged to record highs and lows, then returned to its balance.

8. *In this example, it may be easiest to add a verb to the second component of the list.*

   Early that year, the young poet started school, took up acting lessons, and began playing musical instruments.

9. It is easier to fly a plane than to land one on the ground.

Exercise S: (Other possibilities may exist other than those I've included.)

1. Should the president pass away, the vice-president assumes the presidency.

2. I am investigating three things: the limits of chemistry in botany, the effects of mercury on saplings, and any research that overlaps these subjects.

    I am investigating the limits of chemistry in botany, the effects of mercury on saplings, and any research that overlaps these subjects.

3. Talent is not natural. It is earned in private and displayed in public.

    Talent is not natural; it is earned in private and displayed in public.

    Talent is not natural—it is earned in private and displayed in public.

4. Consequently, the army is becoming a necessary choice for young men and women—no matter how much they wish to enroll in college immediately.

    No matter how much young men and women wish to enroll in college immediately, the army is becoming a necessary choice.

5. They serve with honor, pride, and humility.

6. I used to sing a lot in the church choir.

7. The fountain of youth has never been found for many reasons, including the impossibility of its existence.

    The fountain of youth has never been found for many reasons—including the impossibility of its existence.

8. After many years of drought—and because of plentiful rain—the Irish Potato Famine eventually ended.

    Because of plentiful rain, after many years of drought, the Irish Potato Famine eventually ended.

9. Coffee should not be taken by children because their growth is stunted.

    Coffee should not be taken by children—because their growth is stunted.

Information Across Sentences

❁

Old and New Information

Information is not gathered into just sentences and paragraphs. Whenever two sentences are grouped together, they appear next to each other because they continue a writer's thought. Obviously, this is true for three sentences, four sentences, etc. The farther you get from "sentence one," the more elaborate the information will become, and the more distant the basic idea of sentence one will be. Eventually, enough new information will enter and the topic will be new. Yet even these larger topics elaborate on ideas presented in old information.

This new subject may demand a new paragraph, or it may not. Likewise, elaboration on one topic may take several paragraphs. Regardless of how much elaboration exists, a basic idea rests behind elaboration. Older information always reappears in some form, reminding the reader of what they've been told. New information is added to this, further elaborating or introducing claims, support, and relevant information.

Here are a few basic examples:

John bought a new car. It gets good gas mileage.

Old information: *It* (John's new car)
New information: *gets good gas mileage*

Gets good gas mileage elaborates on the old information, John's new car. You may recognize that old information/new information can be the cause for redundancy. The two sentences above could be easily combined.

John bought a new car that gets good gas mileage.

Yet the new information doesn't need to modify just John's car. New information can modify anything in the previous sentence.

John bought a new car. It took two hours.

Now, the new information elaborates on the time it took to purchase the car. New information can relate to any information that was previously given.

These examples are simple and obvious. They are meant to get your feet wet. Old information/ new information will be most useful for checking the order of your ideas. I have always found it most useful for gathering up my messy or random ideas and rearranging them into a more sensible order that places one as old information and one as elaboration. First, we'll revisit a previous example to examine how old information/new information works in well-structured paragraphs. In the next chapter, we'll examine a student's rough draft and use old information/ new information to trace the missteps in the paper's order of information.

The American worker combines dedication with innovation (1). Statistics prove this true (2). Ninety percent of American workers claim their job as a component of self-esteem(3). Sixty percent reveal they would miss their job(4).

Exercise A:

In the four sentences above, underline and label pertinent information as either "old" or "new." Answering the following questions may help. You may also wish to draw lines connecting repeated information. Remember that new information often becomes old information in the following sentence, like links in a chain.

1. Sentence two provides new information that statistics prove "this" true. "This" is old information. What is "this"?

   a) the American worker

   b) the combination of dedication and innovation

2. What is sentence three's old information? What old idea does its new information elaborate upon?

3. Does sentence four contain old information? Do all sentences contain old information before presenting new information?

After looking at the answers, you may notice that sentence two doesn't seem highly important. It presents new information, the idea of statistics. In your opinion, would a reader need sentence two, or does the following suffice?

The American worker combines dedication with innovation. Ninety percent of American workers claim their job as a component of self-esteem. Sixty percent reveal they would miss their job.

Your answer to the above question cuts to the heart of editing: how much does a writer have to "spell out" to make solid connections without crushing the reader under redundancy? Only you can decide, but thinking of old information/new information may help.

For the next passage, much of the "old information" is unstated. The reader is trusted to infer why the new information is important. For Exercise B, write in the margin of your book what you believe the unstated theme/old information is that is modified by all elaboration of sentences 6-10.

Exercise B:

Yet the middle and working classes of Americans were robbed of wage increases equal to inflation as early as the 1970s(6). By the 1980s, stagflation wreaked havoc upon the economy(7). Americans were made to work harder just to break even.(8)

Jobs disappeared overseas(9). Many blue-collar towns lost their major sources of employment(10). These sources of employment were not replaced by the government or industry(11).....

After examining the answers to Exercises A and B, you'll find that old/new information works in a large number of ways. While this makes it challenging to identify patterns in analysis, detailed analysis is not the point of this chapter. In the following chapter, old/new information will be useful for helping you reorganize "loose" paragraphs and random ideas in rough drafts.

Exercise A:

Sentence themes/subjects

1.

2.

3.

4.

5.

6.

7.

Are the themes/subjects in order? Check your subjects against the suggestions in the answer section.

Inside the Teacher's Mind:

Upon reading this rough draft, I felt that I, the reader, was getting too many signals for a variety of subjects. This is because many of the sentences end with new information that isn't the subject of the next sentence. While much of the information in this essay could be kept, the final, new information of each sentence in an essay will often prepare a reader for what comes next. Let me try to explain this rough draft, sentence by sentence:

1. A good opening: the subject is women economically supporting their family

2. old information: women

   new information: husbands being laid off

   This new information may prepare a reader to hear more elaboration on men and lay-offs, or at least hard times in the job market; but the author never returns to this subject.

3. New information, the title "Alpha Earners," elaborates on sentence one.

4. New information of women and wages elaborates on sentences one and three; the subject is discrimination

5. New information elaborates upon old information, women and wages; the subject is discrimination

6. New information discusses women working typically male blue-collar labor

7. New information discusses women working in white-collar, educated labor

While everything relates to sentence one, at least mildly, grouping information may help. Sentences 1, 2, and 3 discuss women replacing men's economic role in the family. Sentences 4 and 5 discuss wage discrimination. Sentences 6 and 7 discuss women in the work force. 1-3 and 6-7 are all positive attributes. 4 and 5 are negative. Let's try grouping 1-3 and 6,7.

There are many women in today's America that are working to support their entire family (1). Most women are depended upon because their husbands are being laid off from their jobs(2). Researchers have given a new name to the women who are supporting the family with their income, Alpha Earners(3). There are a lot of women who are filling the positions that, normally, a man would fill and are doing more manual labor; for example, working in a factory (6). Because there are more women than men receiving MBA degrees, there are more women qualifying for executive and industrious jobs (7).

Things seem clearer now. We hear everything about women themselves, then we hear about typical women's jobs. So our categories are "women" and "jobs." The two are easily confused because little seems to separate them, but making the fine distinction lets us organize our paragraph better. Similar ideas are now grouped. However, some information still feels irrelevant. *Examples* that lead away from "women supporting the family" may be saved for the body of the paper in a "reasons" section; or they could be labeled as a cause with the effect of women's increasing role in the workforce. Regardless, *men being laid off* must not appear as an "equal" to the other ideas. It is a cause, not an effect, and it is not either of our two categories. Clearly it is information of a different type.

Speaking of examples, one sentence (#3) does not give an *example* of what women are doing in the workforce. The other sentences do. Our "list" is broken. Let's put sentence #3 someplace else and clean up the language as well:

__Because men are being laid off from their jobs__, many women in today's America are working to support the American family. Many of these women are filling positions that a man would normally fill, including manual labor and white-collar work. Higher numbers of women earning MBA degrees has also increased women's presence in white-collar employment. __Researchers have given a new name to the women who are supporting their family, Alpha Earners(3)__.

The above paragraph, with language adjustments, now flows well because we have reorganized on the new/old information elaboration process. Our order is the following:

Cause: men laid off
Effect: women taking on men's work
elaboration: in blue- and white-collar work
elaboration: college degrees and white collar work
all ideas summarized with catch-all term "Alpha Earners"

After tightening up similar information, a writer would have to make a decision if sentences 4 and 5 still belong in the opening paragraph. They could be saved for the body of the paper. Also, if you have been reading carefully, you may have noticed another large flaw in the paragraph despite its good organization of ideas. The idea of women filling traditional male jobs while those jobs are disappearing (men being laid off) makes no sense. If the jobs are disappearing, how are the women filling them? This conundrum doesn't ruin the paper, but it does suggest that *men being laid off* is not an important enough idea to appear as the major cause of any change. *Men being laid off*, like sentences 4 and 5, must be grouped as equals in a "causes" section or covered briefly in the introduction. Elaboration would most likely appear only in the body of the essay.

SECTION 7

Reading For Others: Beginning Peer Review

❋

Knowledge, Research, and Writing

The following short expository and argumentative essays were drafted in one of my introduction to college writing courses. The students were to read as many articles as they cared to, then write a "history of work." My goal was to show how reading, understanding, and "owning" material directly helps or hurts your writing. As we'll see in the first essay, you cannot write if you don't fully understand your subject.

Each writer below has a unique identity that offers both strengths and weaknesses. While each essay may contain a variety of problems, I would like you to focus on one or two suggestions for revision that are discussed in this book. If you were responding to these essays in a peer group, mentioning these one or two issues would be far more helpful than pointing out a misspelled word or two. It is easier to simply fix a typo, add a comma, or delete a word, but you will not be improving the *meaning* or *ideas* in the essay very much. Thinking of the suggestions for revision this book has offered, give these writers advice on reorganizing information, rewriting sentences, and deleting off-topic information.

Women and Work in the 20th Century

In the beginning of the 20th century, women were regarded as the inferior sex. In addition, women did not have many job opportunities. A major employer of the twentieth century was the domestic service, women that watch over wealthier peoples house and household. Also, other hard labor jobs were available for men and women. These jobs included working with machinery in factories.

During WWI, women took the jobs of men in the factories, because the men were called out to fight in the war. The women that worked in the factories at this time could only do unskilled or midskilled work.

After WWI was over the women had to give up their jobs to the soldiers that returned from war. Women kept the factories going while the men fought for the country.

In the early 1930s, more women were being educated to a higher level than before the war. Due to the higher education, more and more women became teachers. The higher educations also increase additional job opportunities. Women were not only becoming teachers, they were also being trained to work heavy machinery and taught how to use toxic chemicals. During those times, women were very dependent on by the the country to maintain everything. While the men fought for everyone's freedom, the women kept the country on track.

In the mid 40s, more households started to invest in labor reduction devices such as washing machines. These new devices allowed housework to be done easier and more rapidly. The development of the washing machine and other new technology benefited women in a tremendous way. Due to the invention of household gadgets, women began to come into the work force in a permanent basis. Women wanted to return to their domestic jobs because of the technology that was available to help with the work that had to be done.

As the years passed women in the workplace became close to equal with men workers. Women were the backbone of the workplace and maintained many industries while the men were at war. Women have progressed from domestic jobs to male dominated jobs such as police and nation armed forces. Not only has women progressed to male-dominated jobs, but they have started to dominate them. Women in the workplace have drastically changed from the early 1900s to the present day 2000s.

Peer Responses:

Write down several things this writer does well:

1.

2.

3.

4.

Write down several suggestions for this writer:

1.

2.

3.

4.

When critiquing an essay like this, you can create three basic categories: sentence problems, information arrangement, and research. Naturally, other categories are possible.

Below is an analysis I gave this writer to help rethink concepts and ideas, not just rewrite grammar.

Inside the Teacher's Mind: Research and Owning Knowledge

The above essay is a good example of how not owning the knowledge of your subject can undermine an essay. The writer needs to check the facts. Some of the historical information is wrong, such as women working then giving up jobs in factories during WWI. This is true of WWII, not WWI. Other historical information is generic and could most likely be true of any decade—women gaining in education, for instance. The progression of women's education has been fairly constant without any major halts or bans. To be more detailed, the writer should focus on any specific new gains in education that happened in a particular decade.

Also, because the writer hasn't owned the background knowledge, the subjects of their paragraphs are not consistent. The writer is "going with what they know" rather than using the same criteria for each decade of this history of women and work. Here are a few things to note:

1. The introduction has a thesis, *women were regarding as inferior and did not have many job opportunities during the early Twentieth Century.* However, this is a history. What does the writer mean by "early Twentieth Century"? Specific time periods are not consistently well defined in the essay.

2. Education's relation to work appears in the third paragraph, but it isn't mentioned in the other paragraphs or as an important catalyst for women and work. It seems to me that education's relationship to changes in women's labor should be mentioned in the introduction and touched on in each paragraph. Otherwise a reader is left wondering, what was education like for women before and after the 1930s?

3. Comment number two touches on a larger issue. The introduction mentions manual labor for women, a type of work that existed. The essay may benefit from an introduction that mentions the types of work absent at the beginning of the Twentieth Century that will later appear because of education and war, the two major catalysts this writer includes in the paper.

4. The paragraph on the 1940s discusses advances in domestic technology for three sentences. We do not know why until the fourth sentence. Perhaps this fourth sentence should be the first sentence. As is, the paragraph is also confusing because, much like education and war, domestic work has suddenly appeared without previous mention.

5. Finally, the end of the essay covers fifty years of history in one brief paragraph, leaving no room to continue old themes or get into specifics.

In general, this essay is underwritten and needs to be researched. It's not just words that are missing, but ideas. The extremely short paragraphs are the proof. Like the essay in the previous chapter, categories to arrange information are absent or random, so the information doesn't line up well. This is the challenge of writing on a subject about which you may know very little. While doing research is not a topic I discuss in this book, I have discussed the importance of reading strategically and owning knowledge. This student's essay demonstrates the importance of owning subject knowledge before writing.

We could critique this essay for another category, **old and new information**, but without a good knowledge base, this writer was destined to have wrong information or information gaps from the start. *Reading* until you can explain a subject to a friend is the best procedure for owning knowledge. You may also have noticed that this writer has a lot of repeated terms which are signals for sentence combination. As a class, your instructor may wish to use the sentences of this essay for revision purposes.

THE GREEN ECONOMY

The depletion of all our natural resources has been bringing great attention to ecologists and economists for many years, but recently has been bringing awareness to the international stage. Economists are extremely worried about the near future because we will have run to near exhaustion of our our non-renewable resources or have fallen close to it, which will cause prices to become intolerable. From the ecologist's standpoint, the main focus for trying to decrease the intense amount of usage or replacing the dangerous dependence of natural resources like coal, oil, and gas is because of the exorbitant amount of carbon emissions that each resource releases into the atmosphere. These emissions are the key ingredients that feed global warming because these emissions are trapped in our atmosphere causing the planet to heat up. As the earth's temperature steadily increases it becomes the key factor in increasing the strength of natural disasters like Hurricane Katrina, increasing sea levels, and bringing many species to extinction. The problem is distinctively clear; global warming will eventually destroy our planet if left unaddressed. Fortunately the solutions are extremely clear as well. We must transition over to a green economy changing the way that we think about energy, transportation, businesses, and city policies.

Peer Responses:

Write down several things this writer does well:

1.

2.

3.

4.

Write down several suggestions for this writer:

1.

2.

3.

4.

Reorganizing Information, Rewriting Sentences, and Deleting Off-Topic Information:

This essay—introductory paragraph, really—is strong in detailed information. As a class, if you trace how old information is elaborated on, you'll find this is a fairly tight passage. Also, this writer really seems to know the subject, so there isn't any information that seems off-topic. The "story" or "sequence" of global warming is clear.

However, you may have noticed the paragraph is an inventory of problems and causes. The *solutions* aren't listed until the final sentence, so they may be underexplained. While my class felt the information presented is good, they felt that solutions creating "The Green Economy" aren't fully engaged. An introduction typically prepares the reader for the argument/solution. Some students suggested that this writer has written the *second* paragraph of the essay explaining background information before beginning to argue for solutions. However, it is possible that solutions needn't appear immediately and could be explained later.

Also, everyone noted that the length of the sentences makes it hard to remember all the information they contain. Editing these long sentences was the class's first recommendation. I noticed that the writer likes to use adverbs, adjectives, and long verb phrases a lot; many times, they are redundant or simply confusing. Here are a few:

The depletion of all our natural resources

*has **been bringing** great attention*

***extremely** worried*

***main** focus*

Overall, the class agreed this was well-written and authoritative. The problems were mainly on the sentence and style level. Finally, reflect on the titles of both of these essays. Are they specific enough to clue in an audience to the topic, or could they include more keywords?

The Limits of Knowledge and Writing:

One purpose of this chapter was to demonstrate that knowing a subject is vital to the writing process. This means that writing from personal experience will often be easier than writing on a subject, unless you know that subject extremely well. Using personal experience is one method of freewriting on any subject. However, writing tasks such as exposition and argument typically require you to write beyond your personal experience. Reading to own knowledge is a prerequisite to writing.

A second purpose of this chapter was to prepare you to respond to peer writing beyond merely underlining misspelled words or even suggesting verb changes. You have to look for these larger patterns of *thought* and *idea* to give good advice to your peers. As a class or as an individual, I hope that you also included basic writing ideas such as identifying a thesis and WWWWWH in addition to reorganizing information, rewriting sentences, and deleting off-topic information.

Section 8

"Just The Facts" in Introductory Paragraphs

❀

Using Your Strategies

This brief section utilizes all the information provided on the old/new information paradigm. Use what you have learned from Chapters Five, Six, and Seven. Although the advice in this chapter is general to writing introductory paragraphs for any argument, the focus is on setting up a literary argument. I have tried to choose literature that will be familiar to users of this textbook, but you may not have working knowledge of these writers and their writings. Still, you may find it useful to compare two basic strategies for developing an introductory paragraph. You will notice that each paragraph contains the Who, What, When, Where, Why, and How of the argument. You will also notice that I have included "down to business" model paragraphs that get right to the point. These introductions are not conversational, although conversational models can be just as effective and more engaging than more "down to business" models. For conversational models, you should look at the essays included in Chapters Nine and Ten.

Modes of Thought: Analysis/Synthesis

A new idea present in these two essays is analysis/synthesis. Thinking at its most basic may boil down to these two modes of thought. An explanation of these two modes accompanies the rhetorical explanation of Essay Number One. The basic equation works like this:

Thesis

Antithesis (Contrary idea/division of idea)

Synthesis of the two ideas

(produces a new...)

Thesis

Antithesis

Synthesis

(produces a new...)

Thesis...

You get the point. Every idea can be analyzed claim by claim. Eventually, each claim is proven true enough to stand as valid opinion (through evidence or counterargument and evidence). Thus, each claim, now reworked and valid, is synthesized into a whole argument. The writer closes their argument, resting in a synthesis after breaking down the parts and examining them individually. The writer has created a new thesis at argument's end—one that a different writer may eventually take up and analyze with different criteria than the original writer. This is all part of the "conversation" of thought, research, and writing.

Introductory Paragraphs: Focus on a Literary Essay

It is sometimes said that twentieth-century literature mirrors twentieth-century ideas and realities of society and self. In an essay, choose three pieces of literature we have read this semester dealing in some way with the American city and show how they illustrate similar conflicts of life in twentieth-century America.

Example Introduction #1

Twentieth-century American literature often shows how economic inequality can affect individuals' access to social and political equality as well. Without the means to rise above their surroundings and the basic needs of life, characters either fail to think about political and social rights, or they have no access to the civil rights groups that could help them gain these rights. While the family from Upton Sinclair's The Jungle *does not dream often of social or political rights because they are caught up in economic survival, Booker T. Washington's "Atlanta Address" illustrates that perhaps economic success must be ensured by a disenfranchised minority before they can request social and political equality. WEB Dubois, however, shows a third side to this equation by suggesting that social and political rights can be achieved alongside the economic, but only if they are an equally important part of the minority's democratic agenda.*

Explanation

My strategy for writing and thinking in this essay when creating the introduction and the argument:

These three works of literature are a good choice because they are each slightly different. The family in *The Jungle* doesn't dream about the social and political until the family itself has dissolved, while we all know that Washington and Dubois had different ideas on how the economic fits into the social and political. Thus, you have three distinct viewpoints. This makes it easier to discriminate—to find similarity, yet more importantly, to find differences. You'd want to spend most of the complete essay pointing out the passages that highlight these three stances. In your essay, you'd want to develop several sections focusing on each work. First, you would explain the "statement" each work makes on the economic, social, and political environment of the city. You would include brief passages or summaries from each work.

Next, you'd want to explain how each work differs from the other two works. The easiest way to do this is to compare only the works you've just explained. This means that first you would describe the connection between *The Jungle* and economic, political, and social rights. Then you would transition by briefly explaining in a new section Booker T. Washington's interaction between economic, social, and political realities. This would be the "philosophy" or "agenda" of Booker T. Washington. You could compare these basic philosophical differences (the place of social and political rights in economic rights) between Sinclair and Washington one at a time, providing passages or examples from each to support your argument.

Next, you could transition by briefly describing how Dubois is distinct from the similarities between *The Jungle* and BTW. Explain Dubois position briefly, then show how he is distinct from Sinclair, and later, from Washington. Last, you would provide a brief recap of how each treats economy as a vital part of the social and political.

As I mentioned, there are two basic modes of thinking: analysis and synthesis. The second example opens with a thesis on synthesis (the economic is part of the social and political). The author then analyzes each of the three, but by comparing them you are showing similarity and difference (potentially, synthesis and analysis). This is a formula you can use for any subject for the rest of your life.

Here is one more brief example using just two pieces of literature. This example opens up with discussion of the literature first, then moves into larger "ideas" of comparison. This is different than the last model, but it is equally good.

Example Introduction #2

Langston Hughes "Harlem" illustrates how African Americans, despite agitating for economic, social, and political rights during the opening decades of the twentieth century, continually had their dream "deferred." With the idea of political rights existing, but a reality of political rights not following, Hughes discusses how an entire minority population's psychology may have a range of reactions, from lethargy to violence. Edith Wharton's "The Valley of Childish Things" demonstrates how an individual may, through the social mobility that America offers, have internal change, yet still be treated as inferior by external society. While "Harlem" shows how African Americans couldn't achieve a healthier cultural mindset because of external circumstances, "The Valley of Childish Things" shows that an individual from an excluded minority can achieve a healthier mindset, yet still be discriminated against by society.

Explanation

Both these examples are long, but the work of setting up the argument is done. In the first example introduction, we receive the larger philosophical ideas that exist apart from literature. In the second, we receive the ideas of the author's writing. Only toward the end of the paragraph do the philosophical ideas existing apart from literature appear. Thus, these two paragraphs are the reverse of each other. The first starts abstract then discusses how literature fits into these abstract ideas. The second starts with literature, then draws out the abstractions. No matter which basic format you choose, after these openings you could move right into the business of supporting your arguments through claims and providing evidence. Remember, the less you explain your argument in your introduction, the more you'll have to explain your argument later in the body of your essay.

While some openings emphasize an example or ask a provocative question, others provide an argumentative thesis with a brief statement on the value and/or the support for said argument. Both of the literary examples are the second type—a more down to business and direct presentation of ideas. The style of opening you choose is up to you. Just remember what is gained and lost through each stylistic and organizational choice that you make. Ultimately, you are deciding where, when, and how you will present your knowledge and argument to a reader that may have either a lot of knowledge or only a little knowledge (as well as interest!) on your topic.

SECTION 9

Revision and Peer Review Go Global

❧

Revising Ways of Seeing and Knowing

Unlike student essays provided by most textbooks, the following long essays are not perfect. I have never understood how one learns to fix errors by looking at a perfect essay. No one learns how to build a house by looking at a perfect and finished house. Only the experience of poorly swung hammers and misread blueprints teaches one how to build a better house.

The following student essays are arranged to demonstrate various problems in either ideas, claims, information arrangement, or the use of sources. The original assignment asked students to write about an aspect of their lives, then provide secondary sources demonstrating that their life is or isn't so different from others. This means that most of these essays are argument by illustration. The author's own life is the illustration or example. Research should support key aspects of the writer's own life that are true for many. Many students papers became a mix of career choice and career information, sometimes for the better, sometimes for the worse. This assignment is challenging because it combines the two *ways of seeing*, personal experience and research experience gained from secondary sources.

Personal Experience and Research Experience:

I touched on how personal experience as knowledge and research experience as knowledge are similar, different, and equally important in college writing in Chapter One. Chapter Two, effective reading strategies, also introduced you to the idea that personal knowledge and research knowledge depend on each other. One large distinction in college writing is replacing personal experience with research experience, which often comes from experts or statistics that report certain ideas more or less valid. However, college writing assignments can vary. Personal writing, the use of your thoughts, feelings, and experience, is a great way to freewrite. College writing assignments are sometimes solely personal writing. Argument and exposition will often ask you to research before writing, yet your opinion will be personal. It is easy to see that writing doesn't really allow you to separate these two halves of knowledge.

The following essays asked students to mix the two types of knowledge. You will be able to see how students tackled this tough assignment. Some essays seem to be missing ideas. Others have ideas that are irrelevant when the writer has drifted from their thesis and intention. Information in these essays may need to be rearranged in large chunks, such as whole paragraphs, or in smaller chunks, such as inside a single paragraph. Some could use secondary source support for their argumentative claims, while others use secondary sources when not needed. More importantly, each student struggles at moments to use research to support their personal experiences and opinions, which is why these essays have "global" problems. At moments, they aren't sure how they are *seeing* the world. Their personal insight and research insight aren't blended into a single idea or purpose.

While I have not detailed some of the problems in these essays because the problems fall beyond the range of this short book, your class and instructor can or already may have discussed these ideas more fully. Once again, these essays can be seen as practice for peer group suggestions that are more useful than simply correcting spelling or punctuation. Reading rough drafts is different than reading finished writing. You do not read for information alone; you read for missing information or ways to connect the information better. *You must try to understand what the author is attempting, not simply dismiss or refute their organization and content.* Before each essay, I have included suggestions on several of the essay's strengths and several of the essay's major flaws, as well as how they could be solved during a rewrite.

My suggestions will emphasize "global" problems and revision strategies of a type that short exercises such as those in a book like this can never predict or solve. I hope that you will be introduced to several reasons for global mistakes through these essays and that you will also note more "local" sentence, paragraph, and voice errors of the type addressed in this book. Local errors are tougher to spot when they are in a paragraph and not separated for "exercises." Global errors are tough to spot because they are conceptual errors that are problems long before the writer begins typing. I have also left MLA citation "as is" in these papers. Instructors and students will want to examine which papers have correct formatting, in-text citations, and Works Cited pages.

I have arranged these essays with attention to those with a strong voice and sense of purpose to those with global errors that still seem to be searching for a subject and organizing principles. I have also sequenced papers that contain similar errors so that exposure to certain types of global mistakes is at a maximum. Instructors may wish to identify which essays serve their classroom needs and discuss the appropriate essays. I would recommend small group peer-review of each sample paper, then a class discussion of each small group's advice to the author. Sections of essays that contain many local errors could be used for sentence-level revision exercises as well, completing both halves of the revision process.

Global Revision Criteria:

1. Is the voice and content (personal experience, research, etc.) consistent throughout the entire essay? If it changes, is there a good reason?

2. Are the paragraphs (and linking paragraphs) sequenced properly, or could some sections be shifted to other locations or deleted entirely?

3. Are there major argumentative claims or opinions requiring support to make them seem more credible?

4. Does the writer leave out important and related ideas that are required for a complete discussion of the subject?

5. Is the title specific enough, and does it contain some key ideas that signal the writer's subject and intentions? Could you name a keyword or two that could also appear in the title to help prepare a reader?

Naturally, you should also look for a thesis, WWWWWH, and other features of any successful writing. Also note any particular local errors the writer seems to commit often. Pointing out similar and repeated errors may help a writer understand their current strengths and weaknesses.

Questions for "Petroleum Engineering":

1. The essay opens up with autobiographical information. Does the whole essay use autobiography, or does this autobiographical way of seeing disappear?

2. Does the theme or subject of each paragraph connect to the next?

3. Are there strong transitions to help the reader connect the themes?

Lyle Miller
Liberty Kohn
ENG102
16 March 2008

PETROLEUM ENGINEERING

As a child I grew up around the oilfield. My dad has worked for many different oil companies since I have been born. My family has moved different places because his job called for him to do so. In present times my dad's job consists of finalizing the oil rig locations. The company he works for fills in the pits and spreads seeds over the fresh dirt. When I was in middle school, everyone could not wait for job shadowing day. All we knew as students was that we were going to get out of class for a day and not get in trouble for it. Little did I know at the time is that I would be making a major decision in my life. Just by going to work with him that one day I would be deciding what I would want to do for the rest of my life. (1)

My family has always told me that going to college was not a choice, I had to go. They explained to me that it was a privilege to be able to further my education. Even though I disliked going to school every day, I knew that if I wanted to raise a family with the prices of modern times that it would be much easier if I had a college degree. For past summers I have worked construction jobs and other odd jobs. All of my co-workers have not gone to college or dropped out of high school. Seeing how they struggle to meet every day needs I know that I want to be able to go to college. Many of them raised there families in places in which I do not feel suitable for raising a child. I want to be able to provide the best for my wife children. The best way for me to start my family off is for me to get a college degree with a stable job. (2)

As I went through high school I did some work with my dad. He said that I had the mentality of an engineer. Many other types of engineers sit in an office every day. I have always been a more hands on type of person. I like to be able to see what the problem is so that I can figure it out. I have always loved being in the outdoors and I know that if I get this degree that I will be able to work in the outdoors. Knowing that I would not survive in an office all day I feel that I am best suited for the petroleum engineering field. I get along with others very well and I would be able to work with other people from all different backgrounds. (3)

I enjoy finding the most efficient way in doing something. With a petroleum engineering degree I could choose to go into three different fields; drilling engineer, reservoir engineer, or production engineer. A drilling engineer develops the plans and cost of the drilling. Drilling engineers work with other highly skilled professionals such as geologists to decide where to set up and drill (Drilling). Reservoir engineers decide how to do the drilling. They figure out the best and most cost efficient way to get it out of the reservoirs. They pump gas and water to fully extract the oil from the reservoir (Reservoir). Production engineers manage the surface aspect of the drilling. They decide what fluids to pump into the wells. They also manage the interface between the reservoir and the well. They also deal with sand control, downhole flow control and monitoring (Petroleum). (4)

Since I will be having a major role in how and where to drill, a lot will be riding on my decisions.

If something were to go wrong with the process it could cost millions of dollars. When it comes to drilling for oil every mistake large or small is very costly. If for some reason the old was not where we had thought it to be then we would have to completely regroup and start over. Everyone will hold me to a high standard and I will have to take full responsibility for all of my actions. (5)

The petroleum industry is very active with all the needs for oil and natural gas in today's society. With my degree I would be able to live almost anywhere in the world. I could go offshore into the gulf and lead expeditions in the search for more oil. I could also travel across seas into foreign countries and search for oil. This could be a great opportunity for me to see the world. I would be able to travel and experience places that most people never get to see. I would also learn about other countries by working with people and seeing how they live in country. I could also work locally and be able to remain at home. By staying home I would probably have to work five days a week. I would also always have to be on call because the rigs never stop. If they it stopped on the weekends then much time and money would be wasted. If something were to go wrong there would always have to be someone on call and since I would be local that person would most likely be me. (6)

If I were to go across seas or offshore this would put a major strain on keeping my family together because if I had kids I would miss a lot of their life. This would be a major problem because I want to be very involved with my family as it grows. If I were to go offshore then I would most likely be gone for a week and home for a week. During the week I was home I would be able to spend as much time as possible with my family but I would also miss every other week of their lives. I would not want to leave my wife by herself to take care of the kids. The way I have been raised is to always be able to provide the best for my family. If were to take one of these jobs I would have a much higher income, but I do not know if it would be worth missing out on raising my children. Money is not everything and I always want to be there for my family. (7)

With a college degree I would be a respected person. People would know that I worked hard in college to get where I was. I am not stating that if you do not attend college that you are a failure. There are many well respected people that did not go to college. Anyone that holds a job position of any sort is worthy of respect. (8)

When I get through with college I will be the happiest person in the world. I will be done with my training. I will be able to go out and get a job and start a life of my own. I will always remember all of the people that have helped me get to the place I am. As an engineer I will always be learning and applying new principle to what I have already learned. After many years of experience I would like to start my own company. I would like to employ people that are in the same profession that I will be in. I want to be able to help people with their problems with drilling for oil. With the need of oil progressing I feel that my job and degree will be around for many more years. Being a petroleum engineer will allow me to make my own calls on how things should be done. I want to be able to work in the oilfield just as my dad has done for so many years. I realize that I have four more tough years of college ahead of me but when I get out I know that I will be happy with my place in society. (9)

Works Cited

"Reservoir Engineering." <u>Office of Geothermal Technologies</u> March 1998 1-2. 06 April 2008 <http://www1.eere.energy.gov/geothermal/pdfs/reservoir.pdf>.
"Drilling engineer: Job description and activities." (2008) 04 April 2008 <http://www.prospects.ac.uk/cms/ShowPage/Home_page/Explore_types_of_jobs/ Types_of_Job/p!eipaL?state=showocc&pageno=1&idno=154>.
"Petroleum engineering." (2008) 04 April 2008 <http://www.reference.com/search?q=petroleum%20engineer>.

Suggestions for Global Revision of "Petroleum Engineering":

After reading this essay, which is well-written, you may see how hard it is to revise globally. What does one change once the essay is at this point? It seems there is nothing left to do but change punctuation, spelling, and other local errors. With global revision, you must concentrate on themes and categories and whether or not the writer follows them. How do you find these themes and categories? Jot down each paragraph's theme, subject, or point in the margins. Here is what I've written down for "Petroleum Engineering":

Paragraphs:

1. story of his father's influence

2. college a requirement in his family

3. memory of working with father

4. writer enjoys efficiency/description of job

5. responsibility required for job

6. description of petroleum industry worldwide and the writer's ability to live abroad

7. description of how the writer may miss his family

8. college will make him respected

9. closing

I would suggest two or three basic principles that may improve the essay. First, the writer opens the essay with discussion of his father's influence on his career choice. Yet the character of the father disappears often in the essay. It seems that when the writer discusses his future family in paragraph 7, returning to his own childhood may help connect all discussions of family in this essay. Certainly the writer's childhood has an influence on how he imagines his future. Thus, the past and future share themes. Connecting them will connect all autobiographical portions of this essay. Second, there are several ideas in this essay: college as a family requirement, the enjoyment of efficiency, job responsibility, earning respect through college, etc. If the writer returned to his childhood and showed us how he came to enjoy efficiency, responsibility, the proximity of family, and the necessity of college, we would get all of the ideas of this essay through the same "way of seeing," autobiography.

As things stand now, I believe there are three subjects going on in this paper: autobiographical memory/father (1, 3), career information (2, 4, 6), and the writer's imagined future (2, 5, 6, 7, 8). The writer imagining his future is pertinent, but connecting it to his past would allow the writer to include his father's influence throughout the essay. Or the writer may wish to switch to a "future-oriented" introduction; either way, you can see there is a slow change in the way this writer relates information to the audience. At first, it is very personal; slowly, it changes to information and discussion of his future. Yet at times discussion of his future is overtaken by description of petroleum engineering.

While the weave in and out of three subjects may or may not be problematic, stronger transitions between each paragraph may help. If you review the essay, you'll see that each paragraph bursts into a new topic. If the writer literally spelled out the relationship of one paragraph to the next, the connection between the personal and the informational may be strengthened. Lastly, the paragraphs on college (2, 8) do not discuss career. If the writer reworked the ideas of paragraphs 2 and 8 to include college *and* the oil industry as a family value (2) and as important to social status (8), then the themes would connect better as well.

Questions for "To Be, or Not To Be":

1. This essay is similar to essay one. Trace ideas in and across paragraphs, as well as the use of personal information versus research information, to determine if this essay's ideas are well-organized and on-topic.

Raul Viera
Liberty Kohn
English 102- 054
8 April 2008

To Be, or Not To Be

Being a doctor is something I have thought about since I was very young. My parents have always encouraged me to be a successful person, and being a doctor seemed to be the most logical profession to pursue. Physicians are associated with qualities such as success, credibility, and intelligence. Growing up, I thought that being successful meant that I made a lot of money by becoming a doctor. My goal of success is the motivation that I use for school and many other things. It is why I work so hard in the classroom, and why education is my top priority. School is very important to me because I want to be a successful person. As I have gotten older, I have come to learn that being a doctor is not as easy as it seems. Recently, when I have told physicians about my plans to become a doctor, they have warned me against it. They told me that I should not become a doctor unless that is my passion, because becoming a doctor does not necessarily mean I will be wealthy. I have learned that doctors face very difficult problems. Not only must physicians deal with lawsuits and problems with government medical care, but they have to cope with making difficult decisions that might result in death or discomfort. Some physicians are also faced with family members that criticize or take advantage of the responsibilities and privileges that doctors have. These issues should be considered before anyone decides to pursue the medical profession. (1)

There are many social consequences that come with being a physician. If a person comes to a physician for medical treatment, there are many potential downsides to treating them, such as malpractice lawsuits. Doctors are frequently sued for many different things, and it is often not by the fault of the physician. According to an article in *World of Health*, "Today, the American doctor has a greater chance of being sued than any other professional in the United States, or any other doctor in the world. In 1989, there were approximately 900 malpractice complaints brought before U.S. doctors every day" ("Medical"). Along with many lawsuits, there are also problems with government medical care. The problem develops when a patient comes to a doctor and receives medical care that will be paid for by government programs. A doctor told me that he treated a patient with an injection that cost him $100. He received a $5 check from the medical program that the patient was under. He said that he had to overcharge other people to compensate for his losses in profit. Some doctors perform surgery for several hours and get paid under $10. Some doctors speculate that every physician will one day work for the government. This is a serious issue to consider when becoming a physician. If I want to be a doctor, then I want to be able to be independent and make as much money as I want. Socialized health-care would limit many of the values that are important to me. These problems have caused two different doctors that I have spoken with to discourage me from becoming a physician. Each of the doctors also discouraged their own sons. This personal advice will have an impact on my decision to become a doctor. I will soon be leaving for Mexico to help poor people in several small villages. I will work with different physicians and find out how much I would enjoy being a doctor. This experience will guide me in how I want to live the rest of my life. (2)

My values and the way I incorporate them into my life are very important to me. If I were to become a doctor, I would be entrusted with great responsibility. As a physician, I would have to make decisions that might result in the death or harm of a patient. I might have to choose to let someone die in order to save another patient. The psychological burden of being directly responsible for someone's death might be hard for me to cope with. I do not know how a decision like this might affect me or even if I could make that kind of choice. Such a decision would not be linked to my religion because

I am not very religious. I am, however, a very spiritual person, and having to choose between life and death is not a decision I want to make. This decision would get harder with time. Technological advances in medicine have made the decisions that doctors make more difficult. Many years ago, physicians rarely had to decide whether or not to keep a person alive with a feeding tube. James D. Torr states in his article that "Physicians have always been confronted with life-and-death choices—having to make difficult decisions is part of the responsibility of being a doctor. But the predicaments that doctors find themselves in today are the subject of more interest and controversy than ever before, simply because advances in modern medicine over the past few decades have given rise to situations that no one would have expected in an earlier era" ("Introduction"). Modern technology has allowed physicians to view diseases and illnesses in different ways. With breakthroughs in cloning and stem cell research, the decisions that a doctor must make will become even more challenging. Being a physician might also mean putting patients and their families in pain and financial debt. This is something that I am uncomfortable with because my family had money issues that affected our household. Because of the pain and tension that financial debt causes, I would never want to be responsible for causing the financial troubles that tear families apart. The lifestyle of a doctor also might mean that I cannot spend a lot of time with my family. Family values are very important to me because those are the most powerful relationships that an individual can have. I would not want to be a type of doctor that is not able to enjoy time with my family. (3)

Because my family is so important to me, how they feel about my decision to become a doctor is also something I will consider. My parents want me to be successful no matter how it happens. They support me in everything I do. My parents would be comfortable with any job I had unless it is sinful. They are both religious Catholics, but they are also practical and reasonable. If I were to become a plastic surgeon that focused on vanity, my family would still be supportive. One thing that I considered about being a physician is that my friends and family might try to take advantage of me. Many people use doctors they know or are related with to receive prescription medication. If I would become a doctor, I would use the most effective treatment methods even if it requires a prescription they would not normally receive. I would of course keep their safety in mind, but I would use my privileges to help those close to me. If I knew someone was abusing my authority and privileges, I would discontinue my help. An administrator for the Drug Enforcement Agency said in a newspaper article that "Prescription-drug abuse has become the new monster that we all face… 7 million people in the U.S. now misuse painkillers and other prescription medicines, up from 4 million in 2002" ("Prescription"). Prescription medication is a dangerous thing, and if I were to lead a family member to abuse, then I would be heartbroken. My godfather was very close to me until he became addicted to painkillers. The prescription medication controlled his life and jeopardized his marriage. I would not want to be the doctor responsible for this kind of addiction because I know the pain and suffering that drugs cause. (4)

Making the decision to become a doctor will be a difficult one because there are so many good and bad factors to consider. The social consequences, my personal values, and my family's approval will all impact my choice. Because this decision is such a major part of my life, I will explore every aspect of whichever profession I choose to become successful in. If I want to become a successful physician, then I must have a passion for helping people. No matter what profession I choose, I want to enjoy my life, my family, and my success. (5)

Works Cited

"Introduction to Medical Ethics: Current Controversies." *Current Controversies: Medical Ethics.* James D. Torr. San Diego: Greenhaven Press, 2000. *Opposing Viewpoints Resource Center.* Gale. 17 Mar. 2008 <http://find.galegroup.com/ips/start.do?prodId=IPS>.

"Medical malpractice." *World of Health.* Online ed. Detroit: Gale

Group, 2007. *Student Resource Center - Gold.* Gale. 17 Mar. 2008 <http://find.galegroup.com/ips/start.do?prodId=IPS>.

"Prescription-drug abuse escalates." Jacksonville Journal-Courier (Jacksonville, IL) (Nov 14,

2007): NA. General Reference Center Gold. Gale. 17 Mar. 2008 <http://find.galegroup.com/ips/start.do?prodId=IPS>.

Suggestions for "To Be, Or Not To Be":

Paragraphs:

(1) The opening paragraph contains three ideas, each explained fully: First, the writer's desire to be a doctor; second, the writer's respect for education, and third, warnings to not become a doctor. All three ideas are explained in detail. I felt that the third idea, warnings to not become a doctor, may best be saved for a paragraph of its own; or, these warnings should probably appear right after his desire to be a doctor. Sandwiching education between "medical career" and "career warnings" may be distracting to a reader. So perhaps education should be saved for later. Education introduces the theme of motivation and hard work. The other two ideas both relate to the profession of medicine. While a successful arrangement of these three is possible in any format, perhaps reorganizing these three introductory ideas would help.

In the first paragraph we see the writer struggling with a global issue in all writing: balancing personal information with research. The writer's desires and his educational motivations are both personal. Warnings about the medical business draw this writer toward research and away from the writer's opinions. The writer would benefit from experimenting with both a personal and an informational opening when rewriting.

2) I think this writer means "legal" consequences, not "social." This small change in terminology sets the paragraph better. Generally, this writer uses secondary sources well; however, the claims of medical underpayment in this paragraph require support. As a class, you may wish to discuss this instance of and other instances of personal experience as evidence.

3,4) Paragraphs 3 and 4 are extremely long. There are many topic changes. One way to sort out these paragraph breaks, as well as relevant information, is to separate personal opinion from research where there is no shared topic. You can always separate paragraphs according to ideas rather than ways of seeing. Your class may wish to separate these dense paragraphs according to idea or by the personal experience versus research knowledge distinction.

Overall, this writer has a readable style and includes enough information for a general audience to understand the subject matter. Choosing what information to include and how to organize subjects as diverse as medical underpayment, life and death decisions, his ability or inability to play god, and his family's feelings require a well-planned sequence, concise paragraph breaks, and strong transitions. Personally, I feel that the closing paragraph gets at what this essay is really trying to do. The first paragraph of this draft doesn't include the criteria of this paper. The final paragraph does. This writer may need to rewrite the introduction to match the paper he wrote.

Questions for "Great, A Geo-Who?":

1. Would you consider the voice of this essay more conversational or less conversational than the other essays? Note moments where more formality or less formality exist. Do they help or hurt the essay?

2. Paragraph one includes a lot of biographical information without transitions. What is the writer's point in including all of this information? What information feels appropriate for an introductory paragraph?

3. There are many sentence-level errors in this essay. Suggest strategies from Chapter 3 to resolve these errors.

Morganna Ochoa
English 102, Mr. Kohn
April 8th, 2008

GREAT, A GEO-WHO?

It took me a good bit of mind changing for my major area of study to land on physics. I began with mathematics, boring to others but fascinating to myself; unfortunately I soon decided I had no idea what career could follow a degree in mathematics. I then changed my major to the ever popular accounting. I had previously interned for Certified Public Account, Ms. Tammi Mitchell, and found the work to be semi-mundane and easy. My strong points seem to be science, mathematics, and details. From what I've found accounting is basically focusing on tax laws, forms, and people's financial lives. After I had already scheduled my classes for my first year of college, I began talking to my uncle. My uncle, being a work-over coordinator for ChevronTexaco, began to talk to me into mechanical engineering. I allowed myself to be steered in this direction mainly because I knew of the multiple opportunities in engineering and how large the yearly income usually was. Although dollar signs were constantly rolling through my head the mechanical engineering course was extremely easy. Fulfillment was not something I was too worried about at that time, either. All I had previously planned was to get a well-payed job to pay for my further education in mathematics and hopefully a doctorate. My friend Matthew Titsworth, a physics major, and I were having ourselves a little intellectual discussion one day. I explained to him that I love learning and I never want to stop; that I wanted to keep learning, so he placed in my head the idea of majoring in physics. Many people idealize that a career in geology would be boring and a career in physics would be demanding. With my plan to become a geophysicist I hope to not only combine the mundane with the demanding, but self-fulfillment with a successful career, the wants of my family and I, and my environmental values with that of the work force. (1)

What does one get with the combination of the mundane and the demanding? For geophysics in particular one may find the combination just as boring as they may difficult. I on the other hand will find it to contain more freedom. As my friend Matt put it, "You can either be substituting variables in equations, or you can be making those equations." That statement right there pretty much switched my major from mechanical engineering to physics. Another thing that I had noticed was with physics I had so many more career choices, unlike a limiting degree in accounting. I myself being a very indecisive person and at least this way I can easily change from geophysics to something like biophysics, or petrophysics. (2)

Thankfully I believe I have found something that I can enjoy, earn a good income, and achieve a sense of self-fulfillment. Not many people can say that; many people do not enjoy their jobs, I want to be that small percentage that does. Physics is a large field with few people in it. A real chance for me to shine. Not only will physics give me that successful career I want, it will truly help me in my life goal. Physics defiantly deals with a large amount of math, particularly calculus(my favorite by the way). I plan to use my income to help further my education in mathematics until I have my Ph.D.. By the time I graduate with my four year degree in Physics I will also have a degree in Mathematics; already on my way to my masters in Mathematics. Yes, another boring field of study to many, but not to me. Mathematics is something I absolutely love, something that always makes sense, the "universal language." People also sometimes call money the "universal language." (3)

An important issue to my family is income. Currently I am making more money than my father, which really drives me to get successful job. When I had at first wanted to major in Mathematics, my family was constantly asking me how I was supposed to make money from that; I of course had no idea

Mathematics was just a field I was extremely interested in. They were all of course extremely excited when I said I changed my major to Mechanical Engineering. My uncle's life, being a successful engineer for ChevronTexaco, foretold the riches which could follow. They had already planned on me getting the ChevronTexaco summer internship and starting big. Of course all of this sounded fine to me as well, until I landed on physics. My aunt and uncle pretty much freaked, kept checking on me to see if I was 100% positive about my new choice. I was constantly being asked "what would you do," "who would hire you," or "will you be able to make a living off of it?" I am sure I will be able to find a job with my degree. According to UL's department of physics webpage, there are multiple places to research at. Places like "Oak Ridge National Laboratory, Argonne National Laboratory, Fermi National Accelerator Laboratory, National Aeronautics and Space Administration (NASA), and Los Alamos National Laboratory" have had many students and faculty from UL working there. After doing some of my own research into physics I've found a huge demand for physicists, especially by oil companies. Also many companies will take someone with physics degree and cross train them into engineering. I also found that I could still get the ChevronTexaco internship. According to ACpeople.com.au a geophysicist's yearly income is usually over $70,000. Of course after explaining all of this to my family, I defiantly got them to be a bit more quiet about the whole ordeal. Thats what I like about physics, it's something I can enjoy and so far it seems to be something my family can be proud of as well. (4)

I am a very environmentally concerned person, unfortunately I plan to work for an oil company one day. While working for an oil company geophysicists are "responsible for finding commercially viable oil and gas reserves by assessing the characteristics and constraints of the earth's subsurface"(Shell). I know just by that statement geophysics still may not sound too interesting, but creating and mapping models of certain areas, understanding seismic information, and mapping 3D seismic maps makes it all sound a little bit more interesting(Shell). I have my own personal qualms against oil though; I feel oil is bad for our environment and so is drilling for it. I will not put aside my environmental qualms just for a job, I plan to help those with their research into alternate cleaner power sources. While working for an oil company, I will keep a close track on features implemented for the safety of the surrounding environment. (5)

After all my changing of majors, and all my own research I have finally landed on something I am happy with. Something that will defiantly be balancing many things for me. My family will be pleased about my choice, and I will be happily enjoying it as well; not only will I be happy, but I have a chance at being successful. I will also be learning to deal with my own environmental ideals with that of my future career's. (6)

Works Cited

Active Career People. http://www.acpeople.com.au/cat/Geologists-and-Geophysicists_2112xj.htm. 2004. April 5th, 2008.

"Courses and Research," University of Louisiana Lafayette's Department of Physics. January 3rd, 2008.

"Geophysics" Shell Degree Matcher. http://www.shell.com. April 3rd, 2008.

Suggestions for "Great, A Geo-What?":

The first paragraph includes a lot of detail that doesn't seem to connect. The writer needs stronger transitions between these if they are all to be in the first paragraph. We need to know *why* we are being told these mini-stories (certified public accountant, uncle, physics major friend). If you read closely, you'll see that the very last sentence of the opening paragraph provides a clue:

"With my plan to become a geophysicist I hope to not only combine the mundane with the demanding, but self-fulfillment with a successful career, the wants of my family and I, and my environmental values with that of the work force."

This strong thesis sentence encapsulates most of the stories of the opening paragraph. However, it arrives at the end of the paragraph; yet the answer may not be as simple as shifting the last sentence to the beginning. If the writer took each of these "values" from the last sentence of the paragraph and distributed them, one by one, to each mini-story, the reader would have a better idea why they are reading. The essay attempts this, but we don't know what the writer values early on, so even when we see these values in the mini-stories, we don't know *why* they are important.

Questions for "How Much Does Love Cost?":

1. How do personal information and research fit together in this piece? Are both types of information in every paragraph, or does each type appear in its own paragraph?

2. Are there opinions in this piece which would be aided by secondary sources?

3. The title could mean many different things? What does it mean in this essay?

Anthony White
Mr. Liberty Kohn
English 102
16 March 2008

HOW MUCH DOES LOVE COST?

Growing up as the baby of a family of five with a dad that worked all the time and mom that was always busy keeping the other four kids out of trouble, you learn to become very independent. During my early childhood years, I would stay in my room by myself and play with my toys or on the computer. Ever since then, I have been fascinated with toys such as Legos. My mind would run wild with the different possibilities that were available in putting the pieces together. At the age of five, I was an architect of these imaginative worlds, entertaining myself for numerous hours. (1)

My cousin Tim and I are the only people in my family that graduated from high school. He has just graduated from the University of Louisiana at Lafayette receiving a Bachelors of Science in Architecture, and if everything goes right I should be receiving the same degree in a couple of years. My family thinks very high of both of us. They believe that we're the smartest ones in the family and have the most potential in the family to do great things. Although this sounds very wonderful and I show lots of gratitude towards them for their comments and actions, this position puts lots of stress on Tim and me to become very successful. The future of our family rests in our hands. (2)

I'm now in college majoring in architecture with the hope of one day becoming a successful licensed architect. Studying architecture is more demanding and stressful than I could ever have imagined. A typical school week consists of many days filled with me going to school all day, working all afternoon, and staying up all night trying to finish studio projects. With a demanding schedule like this, you really don't get much free time to do things like spend time with friends and family, and because of this I really don't have many close relationships with the people around me. The scary thing is that I see this problem getting worse as the competition that surrounds architecture strengthens when I become a licensed architect. (3)

In 2004, the average salary for a practicing architect was about $60,000 (About.com). The average salary for an architect with a Masters degree increases to about $83,000 a year after 20 years of practice (PayScale.com). This is by no means a decent salary for someone that puts their body and mind under so much stress throughout college and their career. This low average salary of architecture makes many money-hungry people stray away from the profession altogether. On paper, the pay is no where close to where it should be considering the high amounts of hours that architects spend working each week. So why do something that is not very rewarding economically? With experience people discover that money is not everything. People have more enjoyable lives doing things that they love, even if that means not being rewarded high economically. (4)

A Bachelors Degree of Architecture requires an average of 4 years and a Masters Degree of Architecture requires around an additional 2 years to receive the degree. To become a licensed architecture one must earn a degree and pass the Architecture Registration Exams. (BLS) To become a licensed architecture one must truly want to become one because it takes lots of hard work over a long span of time. The work does not reduce after school, but actually becomes more demanding with more stresses of life being added to you like managing a family and home. (5)

Architecture is one of those jobs that attract global competition for projects. Almost half of the world's best firms are located within the U.S. with cities like Washington D.C., New York, and Chicago leading the way. The city of London is the architecture capital of the world. (UChicago) The competition in architecture is greater in larger cities such as New York; however the reward is higher because of the large amount of competition. If you want to have the potential of making one of the higher paid salaries or designing the most prestigious buildings in the world then you will most likely be successful in finding one of these jobs in large cities. (6)

About 20% of people who receive degrees in architecture decide to become self-employed rather than working for a larger firm. (BLS) These people work on a majority of the design details all of time as compared to most architects that work in large firms that are only given a certain area of a project to focus on. Your freedom to design is at its greatest moment when you are in charge of your own project. (7)

Architecture is one of the few fields where you can truly make it your own. The possibilities of utilizing the skills and knowledge learned throughout the academic years of architecture are endless. Concentrations in the field can range from becoming a teacher, a city planer, to someone that designs buildings. This enables you to do what truly excites you (Triton). Within each concentration you are able to have large amounts of freedom that lets you control your own direction of thought. In most cases, when an architect designs a building for a client that designer is given a set rules that he must work through. However, even with these restrictions, the freedom to design spaces that give unique experiences to its occupants is there for the designer to nurturer. (8)

Architecture has changed its faced many times since the creation of the world. Architecture was once very simple. It was putting a lintel on top of two columns causing a space, but more importantly a shelter. Now architecture has developed to this idea of designing spaces that make everyday life better, more enjoyable for its occupants. In our world today, with scares of the effects of global warming, architecture has taken the role of becoming the front runners in solving and stopping theses problems with the ideas of green architecture. The future of architecture will be an architecture that focuses on having buildings run more energy efficient with the means of different energy sources, being more conscious in the positions of the buildings, and developing new tectonic ideas that makes buildings more efficient. To stay up to par with the international stage of architecture one will have to learn to focus on green architecture. It is the architecture of tomorrow. Just like life, you never stop learning in the career of architecture. They are always new possibilities to be discovered and current ideas to learn. (9)

I have always worked very hard to get where I needed to go. Architecture would be the only career choice for me, not only because of the characteristics of buildings and designing things, but just because it is so hard. Someone once told me that if it is not going to be hard, it is not worth it. In a way, it summarizes my whole life with just one word. Architecture. (10)

Works Cited

About.com. About, Inc.. 2008. New York Times Company. 15 March 2008.
    <http://careerplanning.about.com/cs/occupations/p/architect.htm>.

Triton College Website. Triton College. 2008. Triton College. 16 March 2008
    <http://academics.triton.edu/faculty/fheitzman/careers.html>.

PayScale.com. PayScale, Inc. 2008. 20 March 2008 <http://www.payscale.com/research/US/ Degree=Master_of_Architecture_(March)/Salary>

The Council on Advanced Studies. 2008. University of Chicago. 20 March 2008 <http://cas.uchicago.edu/workshops/urban/xuefeiren.pdf>

Architects, Except Landscape and Naval. U.S. Bureau of Labor Statistics. 18 December 2007. U.S. Bureau of Labor Statistics. <http://www.bls.gov/oco/ocos038.htm>

Suggestions for "How Much Does Love Cost?":

This essay's strengths seem to be its organization and ideas. The writer is also very concise and uses strong language. Each paragraph stays on track and doesn't try to do too much. However, you may also notice that some paragraphs are so short one has to wonder if more could be said. The first three paragraphs are personal—one way of seeing. The rest of the essay is researched and argumentative—another way of seeing. However, the ideas of paragraphs 2 and 3 seem to disappear for much of the essay. In your opinion, should the ideas of paragraph 2, performance stress, and paragraph 3, dedication to school, appear more often in paragraphs 3-10? Should the personal way of seeing reappear? If so, how?

Paragraph 4 begins the research portion of the essay; autobiography disappears from the essay. I felt that in these research-based paragraphs, especially paragraph 6, there were many opinions that would become more credible and detailed with secondary sources. You may wish to look back through paragraph 6 and identify unsupported opinions. Also, the writer's research may be a problem. Much of it is dot-com research, and dot-coms are seen as an unreliable source for most research. As a class, you will wish to discuss the pros and cons of using the web for research.

Questions for "Counseling and Its Social Consequences":

1. In the opening paragraphs, does the writer provide details as to why she chose the major she did?

2. What do you feel the purpose of this essay is? Is it about the personal experience of choosing her major, or is it about her profession? Does the writer balance personal experience and researched information well?

Amy Guilbeau
Mr. Kohn
English 102
8 April 2008

COUNSELING AND ITS SOCIAL CONSEQUENCES

For some people, the years of high school are the best years of their life, whereas for others it may be their worst years. For me, high school was just as I thought it would be; an overall beneficial experience with its normal ups and downs. I was always a hard worker, no matter the task. However there were times when my grades slipped and I had to pull them back up. My high school experience did help me to be prepared for college and also a career. Although I had no idea what my future career would be, I knew I was ready to work as hard as possible to have it. With a strong influence from my friends, I thought I would try nursing. However, I did not know what I was about to go through. Nursing ended up being the wrong path for me, but figuring out my path was more relieving and eye opening than anything. Soon, I found a new passion. (1)

The career that I have chosen is not only rewarding to myself but mostly to the people I will be working with. Most people have trouble figuring out what you can actually do as a psychology major, but I knew from the start what I would do. My love for helping others brought me to the field of psychology. It's a common belief that the field of medicine is the primary "helping" field, but after learning more about my major, I feel that I can make a real difference. I would love more than anything to work at a children's hospital, much like St. Jude's, and be able to work with the kids on a daily basis. According to Hunter College, "A minority are employed in hospitals, (e.g., the VA), community mental health or rehabilitation centers, industry, government, or in private or community counseling agencies." Although I would be in the minority, I find that it would be the most rewarding. I would counsel the children, as well as for their families, to help them cope and maintain a positive attitude. "Therapy can help kids develop problem-solving skills and also teach them the value of seeking help. Therapists can help kids and families cope with stress and a variety of emotional and behavioral issues" (Taking Your Child). I would perform many different types of therapies with them such as art therapy and bibliotherapy. (2)

Although the surroundings and daily contact with patients that have such grim diagnosis may seem overwhelming to most people, I would love to be helpful instead of fearful. Patients will come and go, and some, I know I will lose, but to know that I helped them through their tough times while they were at the hospital is what matters most. Without the impact of my family and the values that they have bestowed in me, I would not be able to take on such a serious job. My mother, who worked as a special education teacher and a guidance counselor, always had everyone else's best intentions at heart. It takes a special person to deal with the hard to handle situations that she sees everyday. My father is a petroleum geologist who has spent his life working hard to achieve success. He has never been one to give up on anything. All the great things that fill his life were achieved by his hard work and dedication to the things he loves, including his family and career. These traits instilled in me from my mother and father allowed me to have a strong set of values. I believe in working hard, whether it is may be as a student, as a participant in an activity, and one day when I am a parent myself. I also believe in staying true to one's morals and faith. With the career path I have chosen, I will have to hold tight to my values, because of the unfortunate, negative, social consequences that surround my field. (3)

As a counselor for hospitalized children who may be terminally ill, my social consequences are somewhat unique. Although my career may not be harm myself or others on a daily basis, there is still a psychological strain to those who work in such an environment. The passing away of some patients, and the unfortunate critical condition of others, leaves the hospital workers as well as the counselors feeling a complex mix of emotions on a daily basis. Therefore if the moral of the hospital is low, which is to sometimes be expected with the numerous passings and critical conditions, it is up to the workers to help maintain an encouraging atmosphere for the patients. Another negative social consequence is becoming easily attached to your patients. One example is an organ donor meeting with the hospitalized recipient. "The doctors keep the donor-recipient relationship anonymous for the first year, in part to prevent the donor from developing an emotional attachment to a patient who might still die" (Adonde). This emotional attachment is dangerous too, for the relationship of the hospital worker and the patient. It tends to be something that most medical workers and psychologists have dealt with. (4)

Although this attachment may seem like a positive move for the patient, it becomes a negative move in the long run. Some patients are lost, and some do leave in better health. Regardless, if an attachment is made, it would be hard for the patient as well as myself when they leave. It would be impossible to not be empathetic towards the children I will be working with. This calls for me to be a much stronger person. I will have to leave my personal feelings aside and be there to simply help the children. (5)

My career as a counselor for children is so rewarding for myself as well as the patients, therefore there are not many other negative consequences. The rest of my job entails nothing but positive and gratifying day to day experiences. A person without such strong family values and influences may not have chosen a job with as many positive social consequences. Their job choice may involve more negative consequences because of the lack of values or beliefs. (6)

Therefore, without the values given to my by my parents I would not have made such a positive career choice. Most jobs today unfortunately consist of many negative social consequences. Luckily, my values helped to lead me towards a career with numerous amounts of positive consequences. A strong influence for a college student comes in many forms. No matter what the career choice may be, it will always be influenced by either family members, friends, or experience. Therefore, your families values and how you have dealt with your experiences may affect how you decide what career to choose. I have also learned that although I may not have made the right choice with nursing, the process of going through that change pointed me in the appropriate direction. It is easy to see how my change in major to psychology came about, since nursing and psychology have very similar social consequences. However, specializing in youth makes the positive social consequences for a counselor that much more rewarding. (7)

Works Cited

Adonde, J. A. "Recipient and Donor Strengthen Bond Via First Meeting." *NationalMarrow Donor Program*. 7 Apr. 2008 <http://www.marrow.org/NEWS/Feature_Articles/1999/19990820_holan.html>.

"An Introduction to the Fields of Psychology." 7 Apr. 2008 <http://maxweber.hunter.cuny.edu/~bseegmil/hdbk/welcome.htm>. "Taking Your Child to a Therapist." *The Children's Hospital*. 7 Apr. 2008 <http://www.thechildrenshospital.org/wellness/info/parents/22096.aspx>.

Suggestions for "Counseling and Its Social Consequences":

If you read this paper closely, you'll see that in the first paragraph the writer is purposefully trying to withhold information on her career choice to build suspense. However, avoiding details to provide suspense may make for less-detailed writing and not prepare your reader for the information you give them. Also, the writer's first paragraph contains many phrases that lack specifics or causes. Here are a few:

an overall beneficial experience with normal ups and downs

with a strong influence from my friends

figuring out my path was more relieving and eye opening than anything

soon I found a new passion

Instead of focusing on the "overall" experience, this writer could select several qualities or skills from high school that pertain directly to her career choice. In general, these statements leave a reader wondering how? What *caused* this eye-opening experience, and what values arose that created the passion?

To be fair, the rest of the essay tackles these problems. However, even in the second paragraph, you'll notice the writer gets to the psychology major, but not counseling, well into the second paragraph. Although the title includes the word "counseling," it may serve the writer well to mention the essay's subject immediately once the playful, suspenseful first paragraph is finished.

As the writer switches from the personal voice in the beginning and moves into research and information, she is forced to use "I would" statements often. Instead, she may wish to simply combine the information after the "I would statements" and delete the "I" statements.

I would counsel the children, as well as their families, to help them cope and maintain a positive attitude. "Therapy can help kids develop problem-solving skills and also teach them the value of seeking help. Therapists can help kids and families cope with stress and a variety of emotional and behavioral issues" (Taking Your Child). I would perform many different types of therapies with them such as art therapy and bibliotherapy. (2)

may be condensed as the following, without losing the personal voice:

Counseling children and families can help them maintain a positive attitude. "Therapy can help kids develop problem-solving skills and also teach them the value of seeking help. Therapists can help kids and families cope with stress and a variety of emotional and behavioral issues" (Taking Your Child). Although all therapy is beneficial, I plan to specialize in art therapy and bibliotherapy. (2)

Whether or not the last sentence is required is also debatable. It seems to introduce a new topic, the writer's clinical interests. It may be best saved for a new paragraph.

In general, I felt the research and information in the second half of the paper was stronger, and, as is often the case for all writers, this writer has trouble blending her personal opening with later research. I suggested two things to help: First, I suggested more detailed information in the first and second paragraph that connects to the career and research interests that appear in the second half of the paper (a problem similar to essay #1); second, I felt that the personal voice changed between two purposes—sharing her experience of learning and sharing the emotional effects on her. While both are achievable, a writer must be aware that that they are detailing their emotional responses at moments, and simply reporting information at others, then organize their sentences and paragraphs accordingly.

Questions for "Transitions Throughout Life":

When the next writer turned in this essay, he didn't care for it much. He knew it wasn't on par with his previous essays, but he didn't know what was missing. He had never had problems with language in previous essays, yet he couldn't find the words for this essay.

1. Like previous examples, does this essay contains ideas that could be more specific? What are they?

2. Are the ideas or criteria that appear consistent throughout the paper? Where do the criteria appear? In the paper's first half or in the paper's second half?

3. Are the secondary sources used well?

Patrick Fitzpatrick
Liberty Kohn
English 102
01 April 2008

TRANSITIONS THROUGHOUT LIFE

In life there are many things that are hard to adjust to, such as transitions. An example of a transition in my life would be going from high school to college. In high school, these are the years that you learn how to study and prepare for college. Most high school students learn enough to get a general idea about college. College is the place that shapes you into the person you want to be, whether or not you are going to be successful. College is a turning major point in my life. (1)

After leaving middle school, I moved on to The St. Paul's High School. It was an all boys' school and went from eighth threw twelfth grade. I was told this was going to be some of the best years growing up. This is where you make lifelong friends and also learn from your mistakes. At first, you start out at the bottom of the totem pole in eighth grade, and then move your way up as you mature. Eighth grade year was hard to grasp at first, because I was leaning how everything would work for the next five years of my life. After understanding all the rules, I was off to the practice football field and ready to join high school football. I joined the eighth grade football team just like the other one million young men who play high school football each year (Tubeville 1). It was hard at first, because we had practice until six, then it was time to find a ride home, and start on homework. This was a big transition to make, from learning how to make new friends, to locating my new classes. The worst part of all was discipline, if you did not complete your homework; you had to stay after practice to make up for lost time. (2)

As I grew older and became more familiar with high school it began to be a routine for me. Not long after eighth grade football I was off to the varsity team. The memories and friends I made on the team will be ones I will never forget. Not long after becoming a varsity football player, I turned sixteen and it was time to get my driver's license. These were the days that your parents had always talked to you about the word "responsibility". My parents had told me, "we will let you do whatever you want, but when you screw up we are going to lose trust in you". This is the last thing I wanted to hear right after I got my driver's license. Then shortly after came the last year of my high school career. (3)

Senior year at The St. Paul's school, in my eyes was going to be a year that was useless and was there just to make time go by. This was not the case at all; you actually learn who your true friends are and who you can trust. Senior year was a bonding experience for my classmates and I. It was the first time that our school had made it to the playoffs in 5-A football in a decade. The team made it all the way to the quarter-finals, which was the farthest any team has ever made it in school history. Since each starter on the football team was a senior it helped us bond and become closer as a team. This helped us learn things about each other that made us brothers within The St. Paul's community. (4)

By the time graduation had come it was like time was going in reverse. The days till graduation felt like months, and all I wanted to do was leave high school. But today as I look back today, I would not change anything. I am happy with how high school turned out, but I am not happy about my overall participation that I had put into it. I did not take high school as serious as I should have because to me, sports were the only thing that mattered. (5)

Not long after high school graduation, I was like the other 67% of high school graduates that was enrolled in a four year college or university (Van T Bui 3). I was enrolled at the University of Louisiana at Lafayette. This was the time when I figured out where I was going to live and who I was going to be living with. It was hard to think about the concept of living on your own at first because I have always lived with my parents, but it did not take me long to realize that there was no one here to watch over me. I was living on my own and attending college and becoming a young adult. (6)

Now that I am in college, I have to take school more seriously. I have to step it up and do well with my studies. Every assignment that I complete must be finished to the best of my ability, because college is what makes or breaks you in life. I want to succeed in college so that when I get into the "real world" I will not be lost. I want to get as much as I can out of college, so I will be further prepared for the future. It is not that college is overly difficult; you just are accountable for more and have a lot of responsibility. A good example for being responsible is attending class and doing your homework. After learning more about college, picking a major that meets your standards is difficult too. It has to be a major that you enjoy and that you will be working at for the next four years of your life. (7)

I was interested in finding out more about land and resource management. The career that I have chosen in college is Land and Resource Management; it deals with two things, oil and land. I find oil to be interesting and we need it to survive. Land is something to have good knowledge about because the world is expanding and growing bigger each day. Even if the career that I have chosen does not work out, it is still in the business school and I can still have a good back up plan to fall back on. If I were to succeed in Land and Resource Management it would be the business aspect that I would succeed in. I would make sure everything runs smoothly and works together. The downside to Land and Resource Management is that there is geology in it. Instead of working with people, you would work with maps, charts and most of all, earth. These are the types of things most business men try to stay away from. (8)

Most people make the jump from high school to college, they believe that they can do as little as possible just to get by, but this is not the case. Most of my friends have had trouble in college at first, because during high school everything is given to you. That is why in this study finished in 2004, the percentage of drop-outs in college was 51% (Raley 74). Most students attend college, because six out of every ten jobs require a higher education (Raley 74). This is why people who graduate from college receive better benefits for their job than people who did not attend college. These benefits include better pay, less working hours and a wider variety of different jobs (Raley 74). (9)

All in all, college is a main part of your life. High school helps build the basis of your life to come, but college is where you apply everything you previously learned and hopefully apply it to your everyday routine. It is hard to make the change from high school to college; it is one of the most important transitions in life that you have to go through. (10)

Works Cited

Raley, Yvonne. "Why We Quit." *Scientific American Mind* 18 (2007): 74-79. *Academic Search Premier*. EBSCO. 1 Apr. 2008.

Tubeville, Sean D. "Risk Factors for the Injury in High School Football Players." *The American Journal of Sports and Medicine* 232 (2003): 1-2. *Academic Search Premier*. EBSCO. 1 Apr. 2008.

Van T. Bui, Khanh. "First-Generation College Students at a Four-Year University: Background Characteristics, Reasons for Pursuing Higher Education, and First-Year Experience." 36: 3+. *Academic Search Premier*. EBSCO. 1 Apr. 2008.

Suggestions for "Transitions Throughout Life":

Upon reading this essay, I felt that the writer didn't really know why he was writing until the second half of the essay, when the story moves from high school to college. I asked him to connect values he learned in high school football to values that made him successful in college. His answer would be the link for these two stories. Once he had the values of college success, he could rewrite the first half of his paper, focusing on episodes from high school that taught him these values. When I asked the writer what was extremely important about his driver's license and what value it demonstrated, he decided that no specific value arose from that episode. When thinking and writing, the writer was busy filling in the major events in the typical "plot" of high school life, but he wasn't considering which episodes were relevant to his criteria for college success. I suggested that he show the reader specific scenes of success and failure in high school, rather than talking generically about it. This is known as "showing, not telling" in the writing business, and it provides examples that each become a value, like a parable derived from one's personal experience. The writer decided that a major rewrite would be needed. Simply editing the information and episodes already written would not suffice.

As you read, you may also have noticed that some statistics reinforce aspects of college life, while other statistics, such as the number of high school football players, do not seem highly important to the paper's goals.

Conclusions For Global Revision:

While global revision is highly unpredictable, I hope you have seen some basic problems based upon vague language, underwritten or irrelevant ideas, forgetting the audience or purpose of one's paper, and the use of personal and researched information. This final problem gets to the heart of this chapter—the two basic ways of seeing, personal experience and research experience. I have included these essays because they demonstrate the challenges that college writing demands: moving from one's personal experience and voice into the world of research, ideas, detail, and writing with authority.

Final Drafts, Final Purposes

❋

Remembering What's Important

The following essays are polished and successful essays for a variety of purposes. As a class, you may wish to discuss why they are successful. The discussion could start by identifying the audience and purpose of each essay, how the author presents information and research, the form or forms of argument used, and whether the language is formal, informal, or a mix of both. Don't forget the basics: the thesis and Who, What, When, Where, Why, and How. However, these essays go far beyond the basics. Yet no writing is perfect, and you may disagree with certain decisions the writer has made in an essay. Analyzing such decisions will no doubt serve as a valuable opportunity for classroom discussion.

Each essay presents its information and argument in different manners. All four essays can be used as models of successful college writing, whether a personal essay, a research essay, or a research essay on a theme standard to English courses.

Benjamin Ng
Mr. Ryan Farrar
English 101
23 September 2009

THE FLY ON THE WALL

Bright light bounces off the white washed walls, strong enough to burn your retinas, and the musk of anaesthetic and disinfectant, like ghosts, linger around bodies, touching them with its icy fingers. That waiting room was always cold. I used to sit in the middle of the row of chairs, motionless, so I can view the drama that unfolded around me. Stretchers, intravenous drips, defibrillators, enough for all the children in the world to play 'doctor', but I was only the observer, nothing more. This place is the next best thing to a graveyard – it harboured death. When I went to go visit, I brought fries from McDonalds with me, the ones that you pour packets of salt and pepper into, the ones you had to shake to mix the seasoning. Shake – shake – shake. The fries were cold and muculent, and the grease painted the bottom of the paper bag. The shaking was in time with the beeping of patients' ECGs, the machine that monitors heart rate. The shaking was also in time with the ticking of the clock on the wall. Shake – shake – beep. Shake – tick – beep. Subconsciously, probably, I shook the bag to keep the heart beat going; the pitch of a flat line is a shrill and obnoxious one.

Most afternoons after school, me, my father and my sister, would go visit her. My dad never told me why she was in hospital; he always said she was fine, and he always said it with teary eyes and trembling lips. How trustworthy. Doctors and nurses spoke about my mother's condition to my father, and though it was out of my auditory sight, I knew she had cancer. I just knew it. No one had to tell me anything, and I once made the mistake of asking my father.

"Dad, what's cancer, and does Mum have it?"

"It's nothing son, and no, she doesn't", he replied, and though the sky was a cloudless blue, with the sun simmering over the hospital buildings, I felt what I perceived to be a rain drop —a warm, salty raindrop. To keep my father happy, I never spoke of it again. I knew not to, it was a kind of holistic agreement, a non-verbal one. It was almost taboo.

I never cried about it.

Not once.

At all.

I don't know whether it was my naïve knowledge about cancer, or the callow view of death I held, for after all, I was only a child.

After the dreaded waiting room, we had to wait again in the corridor, outside of my mother's hospital room – they had to do checkups on her before we entered. The corridor was always full of charities, sometimes cancer charities (ironically enough), selling arts and crafts, pencil and pens. The corridor filled with charities selling uselessness. We were obliged to buy them. Whenever we finally went in, my mother held a faint smile, struggling to do so for one of three reasons: the pain was over-bearing, or the morphine weakened her muscles and clouded her consciousness, or the thought of never being able to see her children again overwhelmed her. She could barely open her eyes, she was so weak.

Whenever me and my sister asked how she was doing, she would always say that she was fine and nothing more – she said it with a rasp tone, her voice grating, as if she smoked all her life. Her breath held a sour tinge, which always made me quiver a little. She always probed questions about how school was. My sister would ramble about her day, but I would be just like my mother.

"Fine", I responded, and held a faint smile, half forced and half sincere.

When it comes to death, I become emotionless – neither positive nor negative. I remember my Grandfather's funeral – my father was holding me, faced away from the descending casket. I could see over his shoulder and I saw a young girl, around the same age as me, with long blonde hair in the same position. The girl started crying, and I started too, through sheer imitation. I was never that close to my grandfather, and I didn't really know what death meant anyway. For example, I remember fishing with my dad once; not with fishing rods and floats, but with fishing wire wrapped around a wooden handle. I caught a pufferfish, a blowfish, the second most poisonous vertebrate in the world. I placed it on the ground watching it ironically gasp for air, and every breath it took looked painful, making it inflated. I held up a toothpick and aimed steadily. I stabbed its stomach, once, twice, seventeen times, expecting a pop. Instead, it deflated and laid there, dead. I was only kid, and I killed an innocent animal. I threw it back into the sea, holding a blank expression on my face.

That cruelty didn't transcend towards my mother, though. I mean, she was my mother, a real mother. Have you ever experienced the agony of sitting back and waiting? The doctors said she only had a 50% chance of living. Something with peculiar extravagance and beauty such as my mother's life rested on a flip of a coin. And what could I have done? After all, I was only a child. I was only the observer, and nothing more.

I wish I was something more.

I remember one of the many arduous trips to the hospital: the public transit in Hong Kong was so good that no one needed to drive, not to mention the subway system. The roads were filled with buses, mini-buses and taxis, and only those with enough arrogance and cash drove their fancy sports cars - badly. It took at least 40 minutes to arrive at our destination with all the stops the bus had to take, nd I used to stare thoughtlessly at the urban scenery, and admire the natural aliasing of lines intersecting produced by powerlines and the angles of buildings. I distinctly remember a small boy younger than getting on the bus. He had glasses. He had one eye. It was the first time that this sense of realisation hit me – the hospital isn't a place where the sick recover and everything after are laughable experiences with pristine white smile. Instead, the smiles are crooked, with yellow and displaced teeth. It's a place where people practiced false hope, praying endlessly to a questionable God, blaming God, blaming everything and everyone. The reality, however, is that there is no one to blame. Bad things happen to bad people, and bad things happen to good people. Bad things happen to everyone, regardless.

My mother's fate rested on the flip on a coin. Heads or tails?

Brooke St.Julien
Instructor Suzanne Wiltz
English 101-040
4 February, 2010

A LIFE CHANGING DECISION

I want to be a nurse, not just any nurse either but a registered nurse or an RN. To accomplish this goal, I first need the right education, and for that I have to find the right college or university. I need a college or university that will work with me, as well as one that is convenient for me. I need one that has a proper childcare center and one that is near my home. That's why I chose the University of Louisiana at Lafayette (ULL) because I think this is the best place to help me reach my goal.

About a year and a half ago, I was at the Body Shop in the Acadiana Mall helping my friend Chelsea look for a dress to take her senior pictures when I heard this little girl crying. I turned around searching for the cries, worrying that it was my own little girl, Elly, crying. What I found was unexpected and enlightening.

A little girl had tripped over her feet and went sliding into one of the discount clothes racks. She looked like she was about three or four years old and stood maybe three-feet tall with long and straight chestnut hair and watery hazel-colored eyes. Her face was covered in dust and dirt from the floor with tears running down her cheeks leaving little stripes on her face. On her left cheek, though, was a gash from sliding into the clothes rack. I couldn't find her mother anywhere, but that didn't concern me as much as her wound did at that particular moment. I did not hesitate; I just ran to her side, pulled out my first aid kit that I always carried in Elly's diaper bag for emergencies, and went to cleaning her face and wound. I always carried bandages, gauze, antibiotic ointment, some alcohol pads, and Wet Ones in the kit, so I was prepared. I had been worried the wound might be deep enough to need stitches. If that was the case, I needed the mother there fast, but as it turned out, it was a shallow cut that only needed a butterfly stitch or a band-aid. Her mother came running up with a friend or relative of hers while I was tending to the little girl's face. She called the little girl Amanda. Apparently Amanda had walked off when her mother wasn't looking.

When I was finished and had her little face all cleaned and taped up, I wiped the remaining tears from Amanda's eyes, gave her a smile, and said, "You were so very brave for me, and I'm sure you will be better in no time." She gave me a sweet little hug and a watery smile. Her mother was trying to dry her own eyes and calm down from her scare, but she smiled and thanked me for finding Amanda and taking such good care of her.

This experience answered a question I have wondered about for a long time. If something like that were to happen, would I freeze up and hesitate, or would I react by jumping to the injured person's aid? Besides an answer to my question, I was praised and thanked for my good deed. That and the knowledge of what I accomplished gave me such a wonderful feeling and made me feel very proud.

Because of that experience and that little girl, Amanda, I started to consider a career in nursing. Thus, my search began. I needed to discover the different fields involved in health and human services (HHS) so I could better understand what exactly I wanted to do. While researching the different fields of HHS, I also learned a little about the benefits and the education requirements for each specific field. I finally settled on becoming an RN. To become an RN, I would need to acquire either my Associate's degree or my Bachelor's degree. I decided that if I was going to do this, then I was going to go for a Bachelor's degree.

After I discovered what I wanted to do and what kind of education I needed, I then needed to figure out where it was I wanted to go to get my required education and degree. I didn't want to go just anywhere. I wanted to go somewhere that was respectable and qualified to give me the education I needed to be the best I could be. These requirements in my search led me to the University of Louisiana at Lafayette College of Nursing program.

ULL's Nursing Program was awarded the Nightingale Nursing Award in 2009. The only other school that registered for this award was Louisiana State University of Baton Rouge ("University"). This award is "to celebrate outstanding nurses and elevate the nursing profession. The goals of the program are to encourage retention, inspire future nurses, focus public attention, and recognize the breadth and scope of nursing practice at the local level" ("Nightingale"). After learning about their prestige, I decided this was where I wanted to go.

Aside from the Nursing Department's prestige, it had a highly qualified and recommended child care center with a wonderful and caring staff. The Child Development and Lifelong Learning Center takes good care of their charges. The open hours for the center were compatible to my class schedule. It's also a wonderful convenience because it's near the campus, so I could get to her easily in case of an emergency.

The campus was within close proximity to my home so I could commute easily. I live at Brook-wood Apartments in Lafayette. There is a bus stop on Johnston Street in front of Daiquiri's Supreme, which is only a few minutes walk from my apartment, so I can take the city bus to and from school every day, or I can get my boyfriend, Mark, to bring me.

After deciding on the college, I needed to apply and be accepted into UL and the Nursing Program. Within a few months, I received my award letter. I was now a qualified UL Student enrolled in the Nursing Department. It's strange how a simple action or experience can open up new paths for a person and make things more clear. It's something that happens at least once in everyone's lifetime and most people don't even realize or notice.

Works Cited

"UL at Lafayette Named 2009 Nightingale Nursing School of the Year." *University of Louisiana at Lafayette: Nursing and Allied Health Professions.* College of Nursing and Allied Health Professions, 2003. Web. 4 Feb., 2010.

"Nightingale Awards for Excellence in Nursing." *Nightingale Nursing Awards.* Nightingale Nursing Awards, 2009. Web. 4 Feb., 2010.

Kimberly Hillhouse
Chun Lee
English 102
February 2, 2010

THEM THERE EYES

Can beauty really be found at the end of a brush or in a tube of lipstick? Can the simple act of curling one's eyelashes or plucking a few stray brow hairs completely transform the shape of the eyes? The small gathering of women at Erica Dunn's tiny studio apartment seems to think this is possible. In fact, for a fee of $50 per person, Erica—or "Diva" as she is most often called—has promised her students an entire class on nothing but the eyes. Before the class begins, Diva explains why she has chosen today's subject for instruction. "Everyone tells me they want to learn how to do their eyes," she explains. "It's always been my trademark. I can do a whole face, and, if the eyes aren't quite the way I want them, I don't feel like I've finished the look." As a professional makeup artist currently working in the movie and fashion industry and a former M.A.C. (Make-up Art Cosmetics) sales representative, Diva has been supplementing her income by holding makeup tutorials on the weekends she is not on set. She says that several of the women at today's session have attended religiously since the class's inception. Clearly Diva has proven to her students that she knows her way around a pigment pot, and, with just one glimpse of her, one could never doubt her skill. Diva's dark brown eyes are meticulously done. Her eyelids are brilliant in bright fuchsia and smoky "winged" black liner. As she explains the presence of a completely clean-faced observer with a recording device and notebook, her perfectly affixed false eyelashes flutter becomingly. There are a few forgiving grins while Diva chooses a model out of the group. Soon, the reason these women have sacrificed their Sunday afternoon is apparent. They are all chasing beauty, constantly searching for the smallest, barely noticeable enhancement or, for some, a complete transformation through the application of cosmetics.

The terms "classic", "retro", and "modern" are often used when describing art, but they can also be used in terms of certain "looks" that can be achieved with makeup application. The late Kevyn Aucoin, a Louisiana-born celebrity makeup artist, is quoted often by Diva, as several of his books—particularly *Making Faces*—define these looks and make each one unique with signature characteristics. Many of the women at Diva's tutorial are hoping to achieve one or more of these particular looks, depending on a mood, an event, or the type of clothing they plan to wear. Most of them claim that they do not go anywhere without wearing some type of cosmetic, and one woman even states that she "hates herself without makeup." They all say that they hope to achieve a particular aesthetic or a special type of beauty, most often exemplified by a celebrity or fashion model. For example, Lisa, a tall brunette in her late twenties, explains why she has chosen to emulate Jessica Alba. "I think her look is very classic. The way she does her eyes," she sighs, "I would love to look like her. To be that pretty…" Diva instructs Lisa on how to achieve the look by brushing on a very thin layer of shimmery gold eye shadow, curling the lashes, and applying one coat of black mascara. She explains that because Jessica Alba has very large, round eyes, there is no need for eyeliner, and how the effect can be a subtle "daytime" look when paired with a sheer pink lip gloss or a "nighttime" look when paired with bright red lipstick.

Reference photos are shown around the room, and Marilyn Monroe's "bedroom" eyes are demonstrated next. Diva calls this a "retro" look, most notably characterized by what she describes as a "down-turned" eye. "Marilyn would wear false eyelashes that were pushed down a little at the outer corners," she explains. "This made her look a little sleepy, so people started to say that she had "bedroom eyes'." It is only a slight modification, but Diva claims that it can be used to create a look similar to Monroe's. She begins the look by brushing the eyebrows up (because Monroe had very distinctive brows) and applying a creamy white eye shadow to the entire eyelid. She then lines the upper lids with black liquid eyeliner "as close to the lash line as possible." The false eyelashes are next, and Diva applies her glue to the first strip using the non-bristled end of a small brush. To show a contrast Diva demonstrates on the right eye how to apply the lashes normally. On the left eye she attaches the lashes and gently pushes down on the outer corner until the glue is dry. Mascara is brushed onto both the real and false eyelashes after they are curled. Diva then asks the students to gather around and view the model from several different angles. Amazingly, the left eye seems to look "sleepy" or hooded, while the right eye appears wide open. When slightly closed and observed from a low angle, the model's left eye looks nearly identical to Marilyn Monroe's.

"A lot of people ask me to show them how to do a smoky eye," Diva says. "It's really modern and looks great with little or no other makeup." She explains that Kevyn Aucoin often used "smudged" liners blended with eye shadows to alter the shape of the eye and to enhance the color of the iris. She selects a blonde, blue-eyed model and, to show contrast, begins by lining only the left eye with a black pencil at the inner and outer lid close to the eyelashes. At the outside corner of the eye she "wings" the pencil upward. Diva then takes a sponge-tipped shadow brush and gently blends the two lines in with the exception of the "winged" tips. "It's really important to smudge after you line," she says. "Don't feel bad if you mess up! You can always fix the lines with your shadow." Next, she applies black eye shadow into the crease of the eyelid and then uses a dark grey in the middle to blend the liner and the black shadow together.

Diva finishes the look by curling the eyelashes and applying mascara. The model opens her eyes, and the difference is immediately obvious. The iris of the unaltered eye looks one-dimensional and has a full and round shape. The smoky eye appears exotic. It takes on an elliptical shape, and the iris appears more vibrant, giving the blue shade depth and opacity.

Many people believe that beauty can be achieved by anyone with the right amount of skill and products, and the women who attended Diva's eye opening tutorial are no exception. Whether the objective is a subtle and sexy down-turned eye, or a sultry, smoky lid, makeup enthusiasts are all chasing a sometimes elusive brand of beauty. The desired look may be that of a vintage pinup or an almond-eyed Audrey Hepburn, but the motivation behind these desires is the same. It has been determined that beauty is indeed in the eye of the beholder, especially if the beholder yearns to be the beauty.

Skyla M. Wilson
October 30, 2009
ENGL102/ MW 2:30PM-3:45PM
Research Paper 1

BAM! ZAP! BOOM! CLASS IS IN SESSION!

I remember being in elementary and playing that typing computer game that my generation knows all too well. I was so happy to play those games, even if it was to learn typing. One fond moment I have of video games is when I finished a very hard puzzling adventure game. It made me feel so proud because after all the hard work I finally finished it. As I became older, I realized that the puzzles and objectives in the game actually increased my critical thinking skills in a fun way without even noticing and also promoted real life situations. For example, in *The Legend of Zelda: Ocarina of Time*, there was a puzzle that needed to be solved before entry to the next room. The puzzle involved pillars with fans on top situated on a specific part of the floor with a certain design on it. In order to cross into the other room, the player had to throw the boomerang at the fans in the same direction as the design on the floor. For the player, this involved being aware of surroundings, debating which weapon was best to use for the situation, and, of course, solving problems which in this case, was a puzzle. Definitely more thinking than an infamous fat plumber jumping on top of monster mushrooms.

Contrary to a video game being an educational instrument, teachers and parents alike feel that video games make children or the players in general become junkies and/or non productive people. Despite these thoughts, it seems the classroom is becoming more technological than ever, one practice being using video games to teach children. I personally would love this if I was in elementary and I feel this really moves us forward in educational benefits outside the normal classroom. Many studies have showed that video games used in the educational sense helps children go further in learning and develop increased critical thinking skills. This research is to assure anyone who has doubts about video games being in the classroom that it actually would help students since this generation of students is in such a video game technological advanced culture.

Video games are practically pop culture since it has been an integral part of entertainment for over 25 years. Robert Howarth states in his article "68 Percent of U.S. Households Play Computer or Video Games" that video games are being enjoyed by over two-thirds of Americans. It is part of many people's everyday lives, whether it is a full out night of playing your favorite video game or playing a video game on your phone waiting in the grocery store line, it is part of our lives, especially children lives. Much different from children of earlier decades, students of the 90s and new millennium are constantly using electronics every day where much of it is for recreational use. Leonard A. Annetta, author of "Video Games in Education: Why They Should Be Used and How They Are Being Used", states these children as the "net generation". Elizabeth S. Simpson states in "What Teachers Need to Know about the Video Game Generation" that this net generation spends most time outside of the classroom, interacting with the environment, using their strengths and weaknesses, and choosing their own path (pg. 17). Their minds function differently than older generations because of this appreciation for interacting with the environment. So since children of today has changed, why has the education system not? It seems like the only system that has not changed in these advanced technological times; other than computer labs being installed at the most. For one, there is conflict for it to be implemented as stated by Rhea R. Borja's "Video Games Can Improve Learning, Scientists' Report Says". Borja explains that financially, school districts' have limited budgets, there is just pure reluctance to buy products that are not research-based, and the negative reputation that is given to *video games* among educators stop interactive-game companies from researching and developing interactive educational video games.

Even though video games are not widely accepted, few are being put to use in different areas of education, as stated by Annetta, which she calls "serious games". *Immune Attack* brings biology to the forefront by having the student play a teen character who tries to teach his/her immune system to become stronger (pg. 230). *Food Source* focuses more on social causes where the student plays a scientist that has joined United Nations to provide food to a famine plagued country (pg. 230). *Discover Babylon* takes a history route by immersing the student in a Mesopotamian society (pg. 230). These video games focus on main education areas as well as an awareness of the world. It gives students of the net generation motivation to learn and hopefully feel aware of what state the world is in. Scientists feel these serious games need to be implemented in the 21st century in order to have great leaders of tomorrow since video games give more positive engagement to the net generation (pg. 231).

Also, contrary to belief of video games promoting sedentary lifestyle, video games are also being implemented in getting kids on their feet as stated by Josh Trout and Brett Christie's "Interactive Video Games in Physical Education". This is definitely a good sign in a growing population of obese children. Since interactive gaming is fairly new, the more people play the more it may be implemented for physical purposes (Trout). *Cybex Trazer* is a performance assessment game that helps point out movement deficits and promotes vertical leaping ability, reaction time, and power, while at the same time providing a fun way to interact in a virtual reality environment (Trout). *Eyetoy* and its predecessor *Eyetoy: Kinetics*, which is more exercise based, lets the player become the controls of the game by using your arms, legs, head, and torso (Trout). *Cateye Gamebike* is a racing game which promotes hand-eye coordination (Trout). *Sportwall* is used with the *Smartball* which helps promote motor skills, enhance hand-eye coordination, visual-motor integration, agility, balance, bilateral coordination, concentration and listening skills, spatial awareness, flexibility, aiming, throwing, core strength, speed, and sport-specific skill training (Trout). *Dance Dance Revolution* is the more popular of the bunch, allowing players to "dance" on arrows at a given time at challenging time intervals (Trout). Students love playing it, as well as the other interactive games mentioned, and get a workout also. Many people have claimed that *DDR* has helped them lose weight and many popular television networks and newspapers have featured the game (Trout).

As mentioned earlier, one of the conflicts/arguments for using video games in education is the costs. The interactive games can be purchased by the school or instructor themselves or, if money is factor, grants can be given or the school can partner with a nearby college kinesiology department to help pay for costs (Trout). The serious games take more time and more understanding from conflicting parties to help put into action since the games are not fully research based and the reluctance feeling of "educational" video games (Borja). The Federation of American Scientists has a solution to this. The FAS would like the U.S. Departments of Education and the National Science Foundation to work with the video games industry to help research and develop games to improve learning and have it funded by the government so school will not have to worry about finances (Borja).

So now that we see there is solutions to the financial problem, what about pure reluctance against it? It has been proven in the workforce that video games help employees do better and improved work. The report titled "Harnessing the Power of Video Games For Learning" states that businesses, the medical profession, and the U.S. military, and other fields are investing millions of dollars to build interactive *games*, also called "simulation software," to teach and train their employees (Borja). This would be great for college students who are about to embark into different work environments. America is in need for a more competitive spirit, improvement in the workforce, and a better education which video games could effectively help since it engages the student and teaches critical thinking that could be synonymous with real life situations that would attract the net generation (Borja).

Another concern about serious games that falls under the reluctance of it are from teachers that feel they will not be able to teach these games since they feel they are not experienced. Statistically, the average age and gender of the American teacher is a 50 year old woman (Simpson, pg. 18). They can conform to technology but still do things there way, some would say "old-fashioned". Harry K. Tetteh names these people "digital immigrants" in his article "Smarter Video Games, Smarter Kids". Contrary to this, the video game generation cannot go back to "old-fashioned ways". They can only move forward. People like this are called "digital natives" by Tetteh. This causes major conflict and a deep chasm in the education system between educators and students. Some students are not interested in school because it does not engage how they think, they become disengaged which produces poorer grades, and many drop out (Simpson, pg. 17). If educators became a part of the serious game process, there probably would not be so much apprehension on the teaching methods of such games.

While video games may increase awareness and educational skills, Joshua Quittner states in his article "Are Video Games Really So Bad?" that it may decrease social skills. Usually when one plays a video game, the player is focused on the screen and not too much to their surroundings, thus social skills are decreased at that time (Quittner). While this correlation may be true, I think that the serious games used in the educational setting would be reinforced by group discussion or questions from the teachers. The interactive games are used in a social setting since they are in physical education class. Students cheer each other on who are playing and help each other play better to achieve a better score or outcome (Trout).

Simpson states that students of the net generation want to be challenged and make their decisions based on their own thinking. But this independent thinking is something that teachers do not want to give up (Simpson, pg. 18). Who is the really hurting though? It is hurting the students and the future of this country most definitely. The ignorance of some educators and people who are against serious or interactive video games are undermining students that will have to grow up in a technological advanced 21st century world. The education system is not moving forward enough to keep students up to speed with the rest of the world. The solution is that the opposing party let down their walls so that future workers of America are engaged not just in school, but the world itself. A reform of education needs to happen now with video games being implemented in some way. After all, the world is not waiting.

Works Cited

Annetta, Leonard A. "Video Games in Education: Why They Should Be Used and How They Are Being Used." *Theory Into Practice*. EBSCO HOST, Summer 2008. Web. 26 Sept. 2009. < http://web.ebscohost.com/ehost/pdf?vid=5&hid=3&sid=5b443a23-d936-47e0-8da2-934c6f50e3f3%40sessionmgr11>.

Borja, Rhea R. "Video Games Can Improve Learning, Scientists' Report Says." *Education Week*. EBSCO HOST, 25 Oct. 2006. Web. 26 Sept. 2009. <http://web.ebscohost.com/ehost/detail?vid=6&hid=3&sid=5b443a23-d936-47e0-8da2-934c6f50e3f3%40sessionmgr11&bdata=JnNpdGU9ZWhvc3QtbGl2ZQ%3d%3d#db=a9h&AN=22912478 >.

Howarth, Robert. "68 Percent of U.S. Households Play Computer or Video Games - Voodoo Extreme." *Voodoo Extreme - News, Screenshots, Videos, Reviews and More!* IGN Entertainment, 4 June 2009. Web. 11 Oct. 2009. <http://ve3d.ign.com/articles/news/47936/68-Percent-of-U-S-Households-Play-Computer-or-Video-Games>.

Simpson, Elizabeth S. "What Teachers Need to Know about the Video Game Generation." *TechTrends*. EBSCO HOST, Sept/Oct. 2005. Web. 14 Sept. 2009. <http://web.ebscohost.com/ehost/pdf?vid=9&hid=3&sid=5b443a23-d936-47e0-8da2-934c6f50e3f3%40sessionmgr11 >.

Tetteh, Harry K. "Smarter Video Games, Smarter Kids." *BusinessWeek Online*. EBSCO HOST, 17 June 2009. Web. 14 Sept. 2009. < http://web.ebscohost.com/ehost/detail?vid=11&hid=3&sid=5b443a23-d936-47e0-8da2-934c6f50e3f3%40sessionmgr11&bdata=JnNpdGU9ZWhvc3QtbGl2ZQ%3d%3d#db=a9h&AN=42008678>.

Trout, Josh, and Brett Christie. "Interactive Video Games in Physical Education." *Journal of Physical Education, Recreation & Dance*. EBSCO HOST, May/June 2007. Web. 26 Sept. 2009. <http://proquest.umi.com/pqdlink?Ver=1&Exp=10-03-2014&FMT=7&DID=1326854711&RQT=309&cfc=1 >.

Quittner, Joshua. "Are Video Games Really So Bad?" *Time*. 10 May 1999. Web. 4 Oct. 2009. <http://web.ebscohost.com/ehost/detail?vid=23&hid=3&sid=5b443a23-d936-47e0-8da2-934c6f50e3f3%40sessionmgr11&bdata=JnNpdGU9ZWhvc3QtbGl2ZQ%3d%3d#db=a9h&AN=1795725#db=a9h&AN=1795725>.

SECTION 11

Using MLA

❋

- Citing Sources in Your Text
- Preparing Your Works Cited
- Basic Forms for Print Sources
- Basic Forms for Online Sources
- Basic Forms for Other Types of Sources
- Sample Works Cited

The Modern Language Association (MLA) offers specific guidelines for formatting manuscripts and for crediting sources used in your research. MLA style specifies a type of cross-referencing that uses in-text or parenthetical references and a Works Cited list. Below you will find a general overview of MLA style rules. For more specific information, you should consult the most recent edition of *The MLA Handbook for Writers of Research Papers* or the MLA section of your writing text.

Citing Sources in Your Text

When you make reference to someone else's idea, either through paraphrasing, summarizing or quoting, you should

- Give the author's name (or the title of the work) and the page (or paragraph) number of the work in a parenthetical citation.

- Provide full citation information for the source in your Works Cited.

Paraphrasing and summarizing involve putting a source's information into your own words and sentence structures while quoting is copying the author's words and structures exactly as written or spoken.

PARENTHETICAL CITATIONS

MLA style uses an author-page method of citation. This means that the author's last name and the page number(s) from which the quotation or paraphrase was taken should appear in the text. The author's name may appear either in the sentence itself or in parentheses following the quotation or paraphrase while the page number(s) always appears in parentheses.

Example—Author's name in text

Wordsworth states that Romantic poetry was marked by a "spontaneous overflow of powerful feelings" (263).

Hague and Lavery have explained this concept in detail (2).

Example—Author's name in reference
Romantic poetry is characterized by the "spontaneous overflow of powerful feelings" (Wordsworth 263).
This concept has already been explained in detail (Hague and Lavery 2).

Note: The period goes after the parentheses, and you need a space, and only a space, between the author's last name and the page number of the source. Also notice that the quotation mark goes before the parentheses and has no ending punctuation mark.

When quoting verse, such as poetry or song lyrics, you use a slash (/) to indicate line breaks and put the line numbers in your parenthetical citation rather than a page number.

Example—Quoting two lines of poetry in the text
Paul Laurence Dunbar makes a similar argument when he says, "We wear the mask that grins and lies, / It hides our cheeks and shades our eyes," (ll.1-2).
If the work you are making reference to has no author, use an abbreviated version of the work's title or the name that begins the entry in the Works Cited.

Example—No author given
An anonymous Wordsworth critic once argued that his poems were too emotional ("Wordsworth is a Loser" 100).
At times you may have to use an indirect quotation—a quotation you found in another source that was quoting from the original. Use "qtd. in" to indicate the source.

Example—Indirect quotation
Eco says that parody "must never be afraid of going too far" (qtd. in Hague and Lavery 1).

Your parenthetical citation should give enough information to identify the source that was used for the material as the source that is listed in your Works Cited. If you have two or more authors with the same last name, you may need to use first initials or first names as well, e.g., (R. Wells 354). If you use more than one work from the same author, you may need to include a shortened title for the particular work from which you are quoting, e.g. (Morrison *Bluest Eye* 58).

Long or Block Quotations

Sometimes you will want to use long quotations. If your quotation is longer than four typed lines, you will omit the quotation marks and start the quotation on a new line. This block quote should be indented one inch from the left margin throughout, should extend to the right margin, and should maintain double spacing throughout. With a block quote, your period will come at the end of the quotation, before the parenthetical citation. If you are quoting poetry (verse), you will start a block quote after three lines and should maintain the original line breaks.

Example—Block quote of prose

In "A New Vision of Masculinity," Thompson calls for a change in the socialization of young boys:

> In his first few years, most of a boy's learning about masculinity comes from the influences of parents, siblings, and images of masculinity such as those found on television. Massive efforts will be needed to make changes here. But at older ages, school curriculum and the school environment provide powerful reinforcing images of traditional masculinity. This reinforcement occurs through a variety of channels, including curriculum content, role modeling, and extracurricular activities, especially   competitive sports. (209)

Note: Many instructors do not allow block quotes in English 1010, so check your instructor's policy before using one.

Example—Block quote of poetry

In "Sources," Adrienne Rich explores the roles of women in shaping their world:

> The faithful drudging child
> the child at the oak desk whose penmanship,
> hard work, style will win her prizes
> becomes the woman with a mission, not to win prizes
> but to change the laws of history. (ll. 1-5)

Note: Give line numbers for poems rather than page numbers.

CITING ONLINE SOURCES:

Online sources, particularly websites, often lack specific page numbers. Do not assign page numbers to online material yourself because page numbers for a website—which are assigned if you print out the material—can differ between computers; what appears on page 3 on one printout may appear on page 5 on another. If the creator/author of the source numbers the paragraphs of the source, you can use paragraph numbers in the parenthetical citation as follows (par. 1). Only cite by paragraph number if the author of the source numbers the paragraphs: do not assign numbers to the paragraphs yourself.

There is a distinction between a parenthetical citation for a print source and an online source. In the citation for the online source, there is a comma between the author's last name and the page or paragraph number.

Example—Author in parenthetical citation

"The make-believe world becomes a sanctuary. Laura is happy spending hours playing with her menagerie, identifying with the unicorn, or listening to her scratchy records" (Debusscher, par. 10)

Adding or Omitting Words in Quotations

If you find it necessary to add a word or words in a quotation, you should put square brackets around the words to indicate that they are not part of the original text. However, be sure that the words do not change the original meaning of the text.

Example—Adding words to a quotation

In "Crimes Against Humanity," Ward Churchill admonishes the American people to reconsider their treatment of Indians in popular culture: "Know that it [the real situation of American Indians] causes real pain and real suffering to real people" (446).

If you find it necessary to omit a word or words in a quotation, you should use an ellipsis—three periods in a row with spaces in between—to indicate the deleted words.

Example—Omitting words in a quotation

Churchill says, "It is likely that the indigenous people of the United States will never demand that those guilty of such criminal activity be punished for their deeds. But the least we have the right to expect . . . is that such practices finally be brought to a halt" (446).

Preparing Your Works Cited

The Works Cited should appear at the end of your essay. It provides readers with the necessary information to locate and read any sources you cite in your text. Each source you use in your essay must appear in your Works Cited; likewise, each source in your Works Cited must have been cited in the text of your essay. Remember: Make sure your header (containing your last name and page number) appears on your Works Cited page as well as in your essay.

Basic Guidelines for Works Cited

- Begin your Works Cited on a separate page at the end of your essay. The Works Cited page has 1 inch margins on all sides and a header with your last name and the page number 0.5 inches from the top just like all the other pages of your essay. This page should have the title *Works Cited* centered at the top of the page (with **no** italics, quotation marks, or underlining).

- Make the first line of each entry flush left with the margin. Subsequent lines in each entry should be indented one-half inch. This pattern is called a hanging indent.

- Maintain double spacing throughout your Works Cited. No extra spaces between entries.

- Alphabetize the Works Cited by the first major word in each entry (usually the author's last name). Do not use articles for determining alphabetical order.

Basic Guidelines for Citations

- Author's names are inverted (last name first, e.g., Presley, Elvis). If a work has more than one author, invert the first name only, follow it with a comma, then continue listing the rest of the authors (e.g., Harrison, George, John Lennon, and Paul McCartney).

- If you have cited more than one work by the same author, order the works alphabetically by title, and use three hyphens in place of the author's name for every entry after the first.

- If a cited work does not have a known author, alphabetize by the title of the work, and use a shortened version of the title in the parenthetical citation.

- Capitalize each word in the titles of articles, books, films, and other works. This rule does not apply to articles, short prepositions, or conjunctions unless one of these is the first word of the title or subtitle (e.g., *Race, Class and Gender: An Anthology*).

- Italicize the titles of books, journals, magazines, newspapers, films, television shows, and album or CD titles.

- Place quotation marks around the titles of articles in journals, magazines, newspapers, and web pages, as well as short stories, book chapters, poems, songs, and individual episodes of a television series.

- For works with more than one edition, give the edition number and the abbreviation directly after the title of the work (e.g., *Feminist Frontiers*, 5th ed.).

- For numbers with more than two digits, use only the last two digits of the second number (e.g., if you refer to a magazine article that appeared on pages 150 through 175, list the page numbers on your Works Cited citation as 150-75; 201 through 209 would be listed as 201-09).

- Give URLs or database names (e.g., InfoTrac or LexisNexis) for Web Sites and other online sources, which will be indicated by angled brackets in your citation (e.g., <www.newyorktimes.com>). You should also give the date of access for online sources.

Basic Forms for Print Sources

1. Books (Includes Brochures and Pamphlets)

Author's name. *Title of Book*. Place of publication: Publisher, date of publication.

Kaku, Michio. *Hyperspace: A Scientific Odyssey through Parallel Universes, Time Warps, and the Tenth Dimension*. New York: Oxford UP, 1994.

2. Two Books by the Same Author

King, Stephen. *Dreamcatcher: A Novel*. New York: Scribner, 2001. —-. *Misery*. New York: Viking, 1987.

Note: When you have two or more books by the same author, you use three hyphens in a row, without any spaces, to replace the author's name in all entries after the first.

3. Anthology or Collection

Editor's Name(s), ed. *Title of Book*. Place of publication: Publisher, date.

Hague, Angela, and David Lavery, ed. *Teleparody: Predicting/Preventing the TV Discourse of Tomorrow*. London: Wallflower P, 2002.

4. A Work within an Anthology

Author's name. "Title of Work." *Title of Anthology*. Ed. Editor's name(s). Place of publication: Publisher, date. Pages.

Carroll, Susan J. "The Year of the Woman, the Angry White Male, and the Soccer Mom: Media Framing of Gender in Recent Elections." *Feminist Frontiers*, 5th ed. Ed. Laurel Richardson, Verta Taylor, and Nancy Whittier. Boston: McGraw-Hill, 2001. 495-500.

5. Article in a Scholarly Journal with Continuous Pagination

Author's name. "Title of the article." *Journal title* volume number (date of publication): pages.

Gigante, Denise. "The Monster in the Rainbow: Keats and the Science of Life." *PMLA* 117 (May 2002): 433-48.

6. Article in a Scholarly Journal That Paginates Each Issue Separately

Author's name. "Title of the article." *Journal title* vol. issue (date of publication): pages.

Wingate, Molly. "Writing Centers as Sites of Academic Culture." *The Writing Center Journal* 21.2 (Spring/Summer 2001): 7-20.

7. A Newspaper Article

Author's name. "Title of article." *Newspaper title* day month year: pages.

Tagliabue, John. "Cleaned Last Judgment Unveiled." *New York Times* 9 Apr. 1994: 13.

Berger, Leslie. "Quest for Male 'Pill' is Gaining Momentum." *New York Times* 10 Dec. 2002: F5.

Lederman, Douglas. "Athletic Merit vs. Academic Merit." *Chronicle of Higher Education* 30 Mar. 1994: A37-38.

8. A Review

Reviewer's name. "Title of Review." Rev. of *Title of work*, by name of author (editor, director, etc.). *Journal* day month year: pages.

Franklin, Dana Kopp. "*Bend It Like Beckham* Goooooal!" Rev. of *Bend it Like Beckham* Dir. Gurinder Chadha. *The Rage: All Entertainment* 17 April 2003: 95-96.

9. Religious Works

Title of Work. Name of editor, gen. ed. Place of publication: Publisher, date.

Bhagavad-Gita: As It Is. A.C. Bhaktivedanta Swami Prabhupada. Australia: McPherson's Printing Group, 1986.

The Holy Bible. Thomas Scofield, gen. ed. Nashville: Thomas Nelson, 1983.

Note: You can give the title of the book within the Bible as well as chapter and verse information in your parenthetical citation (e.g., *The Holy Bible* John 3:16 or *Bhagavad-Gita: As It Is* 6.26).

Basic Forms for Online Sources

10. A Web Site

Author's name. *Name of page*. Date of posting/revision. Name of institution or organization associated with the Web Site. Date of access <URL>.

Irvine, Martin and Deborah Everhart. *The Labyrinth: Resources for Medieval Studies*. 1994-2002. Georgetown University. 21 June 2001 <www.georgetown.edu/labyrinth/labyrinth-home. html>.

11. Article on a Web Site

Author's name. "Article Title." *Name of Web Site*. Date of posting/revision. Name of institution or organization associated with the Web Site. Date of access <URL>.

Stanley, Sally. "Sabotaging a Child's Education: How Parents Undermine Teachers." *Teacher-Parent Connections*. 2003. Disney Learning. 22 April 2003 <http://disney.go.com/ disneylearning/family-school/relationship/articles.html>

12. Online Newspaper or Magazine

Author's name. "Title of article." *Newspaper title* day month year: pages. Date of access <URL>.

Quindlen, Anna. "Getting Rid of the Sex Police." *Newsweek* 13 Jan. 2003. 28 March 2003 <http://www.msnbc.com/news/NW-front_Front.asp>.

Skyla M. Wilson

October 4, 2009

ENGL102, MW 2:30PM-3:45PM

Assignment 1: Annotated Bibliography

I remember being in elementary and playing that typing computer game that my generation knows all too well. I was so happy to play those games, even if it was to learn typing. One fond moment I have of video games is when I finished a very hard puzzling adventure game. It made me feel so proud because after all the hard work I finally finished it. As I became older, I realized that the puzzles and objectives in the game actually increased my critical thinking skills in a fun way without even noticing and also promoted real life situations. For example, in *The Legend of Zelda: Ocarina of Time*, there was a puzzle that needed to be solved before entry to the next room. The puzzle involved pillars with fans on top situated on a specific part of the floor with a certain design on it. In order to cross into the other room, the player had to throw the boomerang at the fans in the same direction as the design on the floor. For the player, this involved being aware of surroundings, debating which weapon was best to use for the situation, and, of course, solving problems which in this case, was a puzzle. Definitely more thinking than a fat plumber jumping on top of monster mushrooms.

Contrary to this, teachers and parents alike feel that video games make children or the players in general become junkies and/or non productive people. Despite this, it seems the classroom is becoming more technological than ever, one being using video games to teach children. I personally would love this if I was in elementary and I feel this really moves us forward in educational benefits outside the normal classroom. Many studies have showed that video games used in the educational sense helps children go further in learning and develop increased critical thinking skills. This research is to assure anyone who has doubts about video games being in the classroom that it actually helps students since this generation of students is in such a video game culture.

Annetta, Leonard A. "Video Games in Education: Why They Should Be Used and How They Are Being Used." *Theory Into Practice*. EBSCO HOST, Summer 2008. Web. 26 Sept. 2009. < http://web.ebscohost.com/ehost/pdf?vid=5&hid=3&sid=5b443a23-d936-47e0-8da2-934c6f50e3f3%40sessionmgr11>.

This is a wonderful article that supports my argument that video games are positive, if not needed, in the educational environment. Since studies have shown that video games are widely played among students, this article provides information on how to integrate video games into the classroom from kindergarten through college. It also helps prepare teachers and administrators for the influx of video games into the classroom. These classroom video games are named "serious games" (pg 229). The article names the targeted generation that plays video games regularly as the "Net Generation" (pg. 230). This Net Generation brings in billions of revenue to our economy system and video games have a sense of politics and history in its own right (pg. 230). Scientists from The Federation of American Scientists are fascinated by this data and feel video games are the next great discovery, feeling that it can captivate students enough to do their studies on their own time (pg. 230). The article states several "serious" video games that are already being played. In "Immune Attack", the teenage main character has a low immune system, which he tries to teach it to become stronger or he will die (pg. 230). While this concept may seem easy in context, it actually consists of challenging and difficult biological and immune concepts (pg. 230). "Food Source" immerses you into a famine-infected

provided (Borja). This article will show how influential scientific leaders are trying to make

agreements with educational schools that video games are the future of learning. It will show

the conflicting sides of the issue.

Simpson, Elizabeth S. "What Teachers Need to Know about the Video Game Generation."

TechTrends. EBSCO HOST, Sept/Oct. 2005. Web. 14 Sept. 2009. <http://web.

ebscohost.com/ehost/pdf?vid=9&hid=3&sid=5b443a23-d936-47e0-8da2-

934c6f50e3f3%40sessionmgr11 >.

This article states that our educational system is disabling some students from learning

because it is still set in traditional form while there have been many technological advances

in our everyday world. I will use this article to show the harshness of how the lack of student

appreciation to education is connected in some way to this video game generation of today.

The video game generation spend most time outside of the classroom, interacting with the

environment, using there strengths and weaknesses, and choose their own path (pg. 17). Some

students are not interested in school. They become disengaged and many drop out. They see

no point of it. Elizabeth Simpson, the author, feels it is because of the video game (pg. 17).

Children will be exposed to video games, whether they play them or not (pg.17).

Public education has failed to provide for that experience on students learning which deeply

affects the way this generation responds to public education. Teachers, many

of whom have never shared these experiences, face a deep chasm when trying to communicate

with this generation in their classroom (pg. 18). The reason being is probably because

statistically, the average age and gender of the American teacher is a 50 year old woman (pg.

18). These teachers typically do not see video games as a learning tool (pg. 18). But today's

student would love to be challenged and make their decisions based on their own thinking, something that teachers do not want to give up (pg. 18). In Beck and Wade's book "Got Game: How the Gamer Generation Is Reshaping Business Forever", several things link the gamer to a business worker: there is always an answer, nothing is impossible, trial and error, competition and collaboration, roles are clear, gamers are autonomous, gamers dominate their culture, gamers do their own thing, there is a challenge instead of the same school environment which is much different than the real world, video games are ruled-based, various routes to success, your effort influences the outcome, the player is attached to the outcome, and video games creates real life instances (pg. 21). The author feels that using video games as a tool with normal educational resources could drastically help improve our education (pg. 22).

Tetteh, Harry K. "Smarter Video Games, Smarter Kids." *BusinessWeek Online*. EBSCO

HOST, 17 June 2009. Web. 14 Sept. 2009. < http://web.ebscohost.com/ehost/

detail?vid=11&hid=3&sid=5b443a23-d936-47e0-8da2-934c6f50e3f3%40sessionmgr11

&bdata=JnNpdGU9ZWhvc3QtbGl2ZQ%3d%3d#db=a9h&AN=42008678>.

This article states a reason why educators and parents feel video games are making students act poorly in school. I will use this to have information to back the other side. A poll was done that showed 1 out of every 10 children in America has some sort of behavioral problem showing addiction to video games (Tetteh). Students have changed drastically from the students of old (Tetteh). Video games, internet, and social networks are all the norm now and the video game generation was born into this phenomenon (Tetteh). The article states them as "digital natives" and those not born into it but later adapts to it are "digital immigrants" (Tetteh). Digital immigrants have adapted to the digital age but still do things in an old manner, like printing out a website to show to someone instead of sending the URL via email or having their secretary print something for them (Tetteh). On the contrary, digital natives cannot go back (Tetteh). Parents, teachers, and employers have no choice but change their ways of thinking and doing in order to keep the future workers of this world engaged (Tetteh). Video games lures digital natives because the game's primary design is to keep the player engaged (Tetteh). Video games seems like a must for this generation's education since it will keep the student engaged and interested (Tetteh). Game makers and educators should collaborate to make games across the educational spectrum to adapt to the radically changed ways of today's student (Tetteh). Games can also teach important life skills as well (Tetteh). We must engage children of today. Any curriculum of today should use educational video games in order to engage and keep the video game generation concerned and effective for the world today and of the future (Tetteh).

Trout, Josh, and Brett Christie. "Interactive Video Games in Physical Education." *Journal*

of Physical Education, Recreation & Dance. EBSCO HOST, May/June 2007.

Web. 26 Sept. 2009. <http://proquest.umi.com/pqdlink?Ver=1&Exp=10-03-

2014&FMT=7&DID=1326854711&RQT=309&cfc=1 >.

I will use this article to show how video games can help stop the sedentary lifestyle of children today, which is another positive attribute to having video games in the educational system, despite what some say. Educators are inept to bring interactive games into the classroom to help promote activity, which is in contrast to the widespread belief that video games promote a sedentary lifestyle (Trout). Two of the most popular video game consoles are already equipped for more interactive game play (Trout). Interactive video games will probably become the norm for physical activity, which will get mixed reviews (Trout). Video game revenue is in the billions and the average player is 33 with 12 years of video game playing experience (Trout). As interactive gaming becomes more popular, players may implement this new trend to burn calories and fat (Trout). "Dance Dance Revolution" is the most popular of interactive games, allowing players to "dance" on arrows at the given time at challenging time intervals (Trout). Students love playing it and get a workout from it. Many people have claimed that DDR has helped them lose weight and many popular television networks and newspapers have featured the game (Trout). "Cybex Trazer" is a performance assessment game that helps point out movement deficits and promotes vertical leaping ability, reaction time, and power, while at the same time providing a fun way to interact in a virtual reality environment (Trout). "Eyetoy" let's the player become the controls of the game by using your arms, legs, head, and torso (Trout). There is also the "Eyetoy: Kinetics" system which is more exercise based (Trout). "Cateye Gamebike" is a racing game which promotes hand-eye coordination (Trout). "Sportwall" is used with the "Smartball" which helps promote motor skills, enhance hand-eye coordination, visual-motor integration, agility, balance, bilateral coordination, concentration and listening skills, spatial awareness, flexibility, aiming, throwing, core strength, speed, and sport-specific skill training (Trout). The maintenance and cost for these interactive games range from $30 to $3000 (Trout). They can be purchased by the school or instructor themselves or, if money is factor, grants can be given or the school can partner with a nearby college kinesiology department to help pay for costs (Trout).

Quittner, Joshua. "Are Video Games Really So Bad?" *Time*. 10 May 1999. Web. 4 Oct. 2009.
<http://web.ebscohost.com/ehost/detail?vid=23&hid=3&sid=5b443a23-d936-47e0-8da2-934c6f50e3f3%40sessionmgr11&bdata=JnNpdGU9ZWhvc3QtbGl2ZQ%3d%3d#db=a9h&AN=1795725#db=a9h&AN=1795725>.

Joshua Quittner's article states how video games may lead to violence amongst children and their society. The article shows a negative standpoint on video games in general which can be used to back up the opposing argument that video games should not be used in education. Patricia Greenfield, a psychology professor at UCLA, has studied the relationship between video games and intelligence and finds a positive correlation that video games increase nonverbal IQ which consists of spatial skills, problem solving, and the ability to understand multiple things and viewpoints but may decrease important social skills (Quittner). Children, and adults for that matter, do not interact socially most times while being glued to playing a video game (Quittner). Greenfield concludes this argument by saying "It's unfortunate that in our society we are more concerned with raising IQ than with people having a social intelligence and responsibility," (Quittner). After April 20, though, I began to have some doubts--as I'm sure most parents did. Should we worry about our kids' exposure to video games? Quittner questions if graphically violent games desensitize children to violence, do such games teach kids to take pleasure in the suffering and death of others, are even nonviolent e-games addictive, do they gobble up time better spent on homework, sports and other outdoor play, or is most gaming time taken away from time in front of the TV, which, because kids sit passively before it, may be worse for them (Quittner)? David Grossman, a retired Army lieutenant colonel and former professor of psychology at West Point, has an assertion those violent video games such as Doom or Quake help break down the natural inhibitions we have against killing (Quittner). In fact, the military has begun using Doom-like games to improve fire rates, encouraging soldiers to pull the trigger in battle (Quittner). Only about one-fifth of U.S. soldiers in combat in World War II fired their weapons, a rate that the military pushed up to 95% by the Vietnam War, in part through the use of simulations meant to make shooting at humans seem more routine and normal (Quittner). Grossman argues that violent video games prepare players to kill and even enjoy the experience (Quittner). Grossman concludes that he would like to see federal legislation that treats violent video games like guns, tobacco and

alcohol--banning their sale to anyone under 18, which has been done (Quittner).

MLA Manuscript Format: A Sample Paper

Plaisance 1

Brandon Plaisance

Dr. Marthe Reed

English 115-006

25 November 2009

The Forces Acting on Fiction

Historical documentation has served many purposes in the modern world. It is intended to supply an unbiased source for a reader wishing to obtain facts about whatever he has plans to learn. More often than not, however, the author of such historical documentation is subjective, sticking to the facts but emphasizing only the ones which put the author's views in a positive light. Fiction is often a good indication of the public opinion of an incident because it is not restricted to the same parameters as a scholarly historical document; facts can be bent in any direction as per the author's discretion as opposed to remaining completely factual. Salman Rushdie provides in *Midnight's Children* what appears on the surface to be moments of historical documentation, but given their context within a work of fiction are still subject to the pull of his biases. Rushdie ignores certain features of major conflicts—usually ones that make both sides seem equal in fault—and often replaces them with fictional insertions of his own devising. Throughout his novel he casts his home country India in the best possible light and attempts to convince readers that his version is synonymous with the official one by infusing his story with reality.

The Amritsar Massacre of 1919 is one of the many conflicts brought to the attention of readers of *Midnight's Children*. Rushdie describes Jallianwala Bagh through the eyes of Doctor

Aadam Aziz, the main character's grandfather. The description of this compound does not vary between English and Indian viewpoint; both describe it as a regular wasteland filled with people there for a "meeting":

> It is not grassy. Stones cans glass and other things are everywhere. To get into it, you must walk down a very narrow alleyway between two buildings. On April 13th, many thousands of Indians are crowding through this alleyway…. Somebody is making a passionate speech. Hawkers move through the crowd selling channa and sweetmeats. The air is filled with dust. There do not seem to be any goondas, any troublemakers as far as my grandfather can see. A group of Sikhs has spread a cloth on the ground and is eating, seated around it…. Aziz penetrates the heart of the crowd, as Brigadier R. E. Dyer arrives at the entrance to the alleyway, followed by fifty crack troops. (Rushdie 33-4)

The major differences between the Indian and the British sequences of events involve what happens soon after Dyer's arrival. To the Indians, Rushdie in particular, Dyer ordered his troops to open fire on the unarmed crowd without giving any warning or order to disband the "meeting." Initially the British stand was that Dyer "had been 'confronted by a revolutionary army' and had been obliged 'to teach a moral lesson to the Punjab'" (Manchester 692). The crowd in the compound as described by Rushdie, however, did not appear to be gathering as a revolutionary army—"there do not seem to be…any troublemakers"—and was later described as "unarmed and peaceable" (Sayer 132). The crowd had gathered mostly to protest the actions of the Anglo-Indian government of the Punjab district, especially concerning the Rowlatt Acts, the arrest and deportation of Drs. Satyapal and Kitchlew, and the shootings of April 10th. Sayer claims "Dyer's shooting was not necessitated, in any military sense, by the situation in Amritsar" (138) for no violence had broken out since April 10th. On that day, however, another crowd, larger than the one that gathered three days later in Jallianwala Bagh, had gathered at the initial news of the deportation of the doctors who had organized two hartals. Though the congregation began as a peaceful protest, two areas became scenes of bloodshed as Indians swelled at the Civil Lines, and British troops fired upon them. Soon after this rioting began, leaving many buildings looted and burned down and five Anglo-Indians beaten to death. It was in this atmosphere that Dyer arrived in Amritsar; in the midst of this scale of protest he may have felt action was necessary, though his was proven to be excessive (Sayer, passim 136-8).

One of the surprising similarities between Rushdie's account and official British records is the number of rounds fired by Dyer's men and, more surprising, of the dead and wounded on April 13th. Rushdie claims that of the "one thousand six hundred fifty rounds… one thousand five hundred sixteen found their mark, killing or wounding some person" (34). British records agree with the number of rounds fired, but most have the number of dead and wounded as much higher; Manchester states that there were "379 dead and over 1,500 wounded" (692). These similarities are surprising because, as Sayer stereotypically declares, "Indian estimates are much higher" (131).

In the aftermath of the Massacre, "the brigadier was promoted to major general, retired, and placed on the inactive list." This ironically "made him a martyr to millions of Englishmen. Senior British officers applauded his suppression of 'another Indian Mutiny'" (Manchester 692-3). Most of Dyer's supporters saw the Amritsar Massacre as Dyer himself did: "my duty—my horrible, dirty duty" (Sayer 134). Rushdie's concluding sentence to this section seems to echo these initial British sentiments: "'Good shooting,' Dyer tells his men, 'we have done a jolly good thing'" (34). It is important to note, however, that these opinions are no longer associated with the majority of Great Britain, and credit for the change of heart goes to Winston Churchill.

The case of now retired Major General Dyer was heard before the House of Commons on July 8, 1920. Churchill was asked to speak on behalf of the government. He started his speech to the Commons by calling for "a calm spirit, avoiding passion and avoiding attempts to excite prejudice" (*Hansard* 1719-20) because many strong emotions had crept into the debate, including anti-Semitic notions and perceptions of how what should be done in Russia and Ireland paralleled the situation in India. His description of the Amritsar Massacre is one of the most quoted concerning the incident:

> "That is an episode which appears to me to be without precedent or parallel in the modern history of the British Empire. It is an event of an entirely different order from any of those tragical occurrences which take place when troops are brought into collision with the civil population. It is an extraordinary event, a monstrous event, an event which stands in singular and sinister isolation. [sic]" (Churchill cited in *Hansard* clm. 1725)

Churchill goes on to say that Dyer came to the wrong conclusion concerning the situation in Amritsar, citing that "the chief characteristic of [a revolutionary] army…is that it is armed", but that "this crowd was unarmed" (Churchill cited in *Hansard* 1726). He concludes that Dyer's decision process was not one of duty but of frightfulness, and "Frightfullness is not a remedy known to the British pharmacopoeia [sic]" (Churchill cited in *Hansard* 1728). Churchill significantly turned the Commons to vote in favor of the government, which they did 247 to 37. Without this speech England could very well have continued to back up Dyer as his superiors did; however, Rushdie never discusses Churchill's contribution to the British response of this massacre. Rushdie chooses to ignore the aftermath of the Massacre and stay focused on the events leading up to it and of course the incident itself; he never discusses how close the British may have been to repeating Amritsar somewhere else.

Another of the major conflicts of India's history found within *Midnight's Children* is the Indo-Pakistani War of 1965. This war was "fought over Kashmir and started without a formal declaration of war" (Ganguly 1). The first major battle occurred on August 14, and engagements continued to escalate as each side would retaliate to some meager forward progress of the other. A strong Pakistani thrust on the Punjab caused Indian forces to call in air support, and "Pakistan retaliated on September 2 with its own air strikes in both Kashmir and Punjab" (Ganguly 1). As the war approached an eventual stalemate, the United Nations Security Council "passed a resolution on September 20 that called for a cease-fire" (Ganguly 1). This relatively quick war was officially aimed toward control of Kashmir, but the novel's main character says the reasons for the war were much simpler:

> Let me state this quite unequivocally: it is my firm conviction that the hidden purpose of
> the Indo-Pakistani war of 1965 was nothing more or less than the elimination of my
> benighted family from the face of the earth. In order to understand the recent history of
> our times, it is only necessary to examine the bombing-pattern of that war with an
> analytical, unprejudiced eye (Rushdie 386).

Saleem Sinai's straightforward intentions for the war seem quite farfetched. That an eighteen-year-old boy's family is the sole basis for two countries to go to war is improbable at best, yet Rushdie makes this fantastic claim sound like a very possible reality, the very definition of Magic Realism. The recurring connected-to-India idea is strongly emphasized throughout this passage: "if [his family was] to be purified, something on the scale of what followed was probably necessary" (Rushdie 387); in other words, in order to destroy part of Saleem, it is necessary to destroy part of India, which the war effectively accomplishes for both.

A small portion of the Indo-Pakistani War of 1965 is fought in the Rann of Kutch, "a sparsely inhabited region along the south-western Indo-Pakistani border" (*India-Pakistan*). It "had been 'disputed territory'; although, in practice, neither side had much heart for the dispute" (Rushdie 383). Pakistan had placed a series of border posts along the Rann, and on April 9th, 1965, many of these were occupied by the Indian Army. A Pakistani force attempted to take back the posts and engaged in a struggle that lasted until July 1st. Many rumors float around the Rann of Kutch, including:

> legends of terrible things which happened in this amphibious zone, of demonic sea-beasts with glowing eyes, of fish-women who lay with their fishy heads underwater, breathing, while their perfectly-formed and naked human lower halves lay on shore, tempting the unwary into fatal sexual acts, because it was well known that nobody may love a fish-woman and live (Rushdie 383-4).

These claims are—as Rushdie admits—"as likely to be true as anything; as anything, that is to say, except what we were officially told" (383). This statement effectively makes Saleem's recapitulation of Zafar's first-hand account the only reliable source on what the Rann of Kutch was actually like, if his claims are to be taken seriously. These claims include that the Rann is haunted not by phantoms and demons, but by smugglers operating under a general in the Pakistani Army, and it is this knowledge that prompts Zafar to take a lifetime's worth of humiliations out on the general—his father—by slitting the general's throat. In this section Rushdie takes a well-known battleground and mystifies it by inserting the fantastic myths of lore with the intention of forcing the suspension of disbelief upon readers, setting up Saleem's connection to the Indo-Pakistani War of 1965, which is more plausible by comparison.

   The War for Bangladeshi Independence of 1971 was initiated entirely by Pakistani rulers, the overseers of soon-to-be Bangladesh. Leaders of West Pakistan seemed to display "indifference to the plight of Bengali victims [of a natural disaster, which] caused a great deal of animosity" (Blood 1) towards West Pakistan in general. Mujib, the leader of East Pakistan, said in response to their disregard that "the feeling now pervades . . . every village, home, and slum that we must rule ourselves. We must make the decisions that matter. We will no longer suffer arbitrary rule by bureaucrats, capitalists, and feudal interests of West Pakistan" (Blood 1). Talks between East and West Pakistani leaders to make another attempt at unity collapsed on March 25th. That same night "the Pakistan Army launched a terror campaign calculated to intimidate the Bengalis into submission. Within hours a wholesale slaughter had commenced in Dhaka, with the heaviest attacks concentrated on the University of Dhaka and the Hindu area of the old town" (Blood 1). It is at this point that Saleem returns from purity into history, though now he is a member of an elite tracking squad for the West Pakistani government. It is reported that Mujib was captured and flown to West Pakistan for incarceration, but Rushdie takes it a step further, stating that "when Mujib was arrested, it was [Saleem] who sniffed him out" (409). This is another example of the fantastic creeping into his novel; a human with the ability to sniff out a trail is fairly miraculous. On the whole this passage is metaphoric of Rushdie's opinion of Pakistan's effect on India; Pakistan's "slippery grasp of reality" confuses Saleem into joining their army in the same way that it contrasts India's "highly-spiced nonconformity" and leads to the two countries' ongoing conflict. It presents West Pakistan in a negative light, which—given that India eventually gives aid to East Pakistan—presents India in a positive light.

   Historical fictions show the subtleties of public opinion concerning the topic up for discussion and receive their plausibility though the addition of certain details of the actual events they chronicle. Rushdie's *Midnight's Children* is a good example of this. The Amritsar massacre was a scandal in which Dyer and his superiors are held primarily responsible, but Rushdie casts all of England in this negative light by ignoring Churchill's support and emphasizing the barbarism of the incident in Jallianwala Bagh. The causes of Indo-Pakistani War of 1965 are altered by Rushdie from a dispute over "the-Perfect-Valley" into simply the semi-complete annihilation of Saleem's family and the purification of Saleem of all past and present recollections. Even the Rann of Kutch becomes exaggerated for the effect of making incredible war rationales believable. Rushdie's editing process of the history of his country through *Midnight's Children* shows his views on many of the issues that have faced India over the years as most examples of historical fiction do.

Works Cited

Blood, Peter R. *Bangladesh: Country Studies*. Library of Congress, September 1988. Web. 4

    December 2009.

Ganguly, Sumit. *India: Country Studies*. Library of Congress, September 1995. Web. 3

    December 2009.

Hansard, 5th ser. (Commons), cxxxi, cols. 1719-34.

India-Pakistan: Troubled Relations. BBC News. Web. 3 December 2009.

Manchester, William. *The Last Lion: Winston Spencer Churchill Visions of Glory 1874-

    1932*. Sphere Books Ltd., 1983. Print.

Rushdie, Salman. *Midnight's Children*. New York: Random House Trade Paperbacks, 2006.

    Print.

Sayer, Derek. "British Reaction to the Amritsar Massacre 1919-1920." *Past & Present*, No.

    131 (May 1991): 130-164. Print.

Chapter Five

Searchers:
A Quick Guide to Research
and Documentation

❄

Section 1: Getting Started

In the United States, we benefit from the centuries-old tradition of free access to information. Traditionally, libraries have been places where individuals could locate data and texts on almost any topic. Indeed, the concept "library" means collections of texts and other materials. Because of open libraries, one did not have to be rich or powerful to have access to information. People of modest means could examine books and other materials they could not afford to purchase. Today, the development of computers and the Internet have vastly extended the idea of free access to information.

What knowledge defines a well-educated person is changing because of the information revolution. The trend is away from memorization and toward what is called "information literacy" which means that one possesses set skills needed to find, retrieve, analyze, and use information.

In some ways, today is a great time to be a college student researcher. Information from around the world is available with a few clicks of a computer mouse. The list of resources is virtually endless: email, computerized card catalogs, library databases, Web sites, and so on. Entire companies exist to develop easier ways to find information. But therein lies the problem— what appears to be the entire knowledge base of human history is available through a computer connected to the Internet. Some have called this information overload "data smog" because the immensity of data can actually obscure the needed information. When faced with the endless information available from books, periodicals, the Internet, television, etc., it may be helpful to remember three things:

- Research on the Internet is more complicated than just entering a few key words in a search engine. Knowing a few techniques described in this book can greatly increase your chances of finding good information through search engines and directories.

- You cannot find everything on the Internet through search engines and directories. An immense "invisible Web" of information, including subject-specific databases and periodicals, must be accessed through gateway Web pages.

- Not everything is on the Internet. Copyright protection prevents much current information published in books or periodicals from being posted on the Internet. Using your college library is essential in a quality research process— both the computerized card catalog and the computerized databases.

Research Sources Professors Expect

You have been assigned a research paper or project. What does your professor expect of you? First of all, that you understand the assignment: What specifically does your professor want you to research? Do you have instructions about what kinds of sources your professor wants? Are restrictions put on what Internet or database sources you can use? Possibly, your instructor has specified that you need to use books, journals, major magazines and newspapers, and certain Web-based information. This means that you are to use reputable sources to obtain a balanced, impartial viewpoint about your topic. So, how do you find these sources?

- **Books:** College libraries collect scholarly books that are carefully researched and reviewed by authorities in the book's field. Look for recently published books rather than older books, even if they are on your topic. Locate scholarly books through the computerized catalog at your college (See Chapter 2).

- **Scholarly journals:** Your instructor means peer-reviewed journals in which the authors have documented their sources. Your library should have print indexes to journals in which you can look up your topic. You may also be able to find journal articles— sometimes in full text—through the online databases offered by your college library (See Chapter 2). For example, try JSTOR: Electronic Journal Archive which offers full-text versions of more than 300 journals in a variety of fields or Academic Search Premier, which indexes more than 4,000 journals, magazines, and newspapers.

- **Major magazines and newspapers:** You can locate full-text articles directly from the online versions of major print magazines and newspapers (See Chapter 4). Often, these publications charge a fee for articles not published recently. However, you can often find the same articles free through library databases (See Chapter 2).

- **Web-based information:** The problem with Web-based information is that anyone with some knowledge of computers can put up a Web site on the Internet. Thus, information from Web sites must be carefully evaluated as to author, publishing organization, etc. (see section in this chapter on How to Evaluate Web Sources). One way to deal with this problem is to find Web information through the librarian-generated indexes and search engines which screen Web sites for credibility (See Chapter 3). Another is to access databases maintained by credible organizations such as the National Institutes of Health, Bureau of the Census, etc. (See Chapter 4).

As you use the methods above to find sources for your paper or project, realize that your topic inflAs you use the methods above to find sources for your paper or project, realize that your topic influences your choice of reference materials. If you are writing about a literary topic such as Shakespeare's Othello, you will find a number of relevant books and journal articles. If your topic is more contemporary, such as the current status of the Space Shuttle flights, you may be able to find some books or journal articles for background information, but you will need to use recent magazine and newspaper articles to find the latest information.

As you examine your sources, remember that gathering the information should help you discover what you think about your topic, not just what others think. This will enable you to create a paper based on your ideas and opinions, with source materials supporting your position.

Make a Research Plan

Will you be using the Internet simply as one research tool along with print texts? For many topics, some of the most current information can be found electronically, and it can greatly enhance your information collection. Will you be gathering all your information from the Internet? Not all topics have equal coverage on the Internet, but for many subjects (if your instructor agrees), you can collect everything you need without leaving your computer terminal.

When making a research plan, you need to consider your assignment. Does it say, "Write an argumentative essay about an environmental problem such as toxic waste or acid rain?" If so, you know you need to narrow the topic from the environment in general to a more specific topic such as toxic waste. Perhaps narrow it to an even more specific topic such as programs for nuclear waste disposal or the recycling of environmentally damaging substances. If you aren't sure what specific topic interests you, you will need to look first at some general sources about the environment to help you choose a topic. Several research resources on the Web can help you narrow a topic and then gather information about it.

For example, connect to Hot Paper Topics at http://library. sau.edu/bestinfo/Hot/hotindex. htm, and find links to references collected by librarians at the O'Keefe Library on popular paper topics such as affirmative action and school vouchers. Browse through the subject links, and you may find a topic that interests you. Then you can do additional research on the topic using other types of electronic resources discussed in this book. See also other librarian-reviewed indexes and search engines in Chapter 2, which also can be used for topic exploration.

Once you have decided on a narrow topic, you can use other subject indexes, keyword search engines, full-text databases, and media links to find additional resources. As you locate resources, assemble them in a working bibliography, which will help you keep track of them as potential resources. Remember that research is a recursive process. As you explore sources, you may find yourself changing the narrow topic you have selected, and this will require you to find additional sources. Even when you reach the writing stage of your project, you still may need to locate information sources to fill holes in your argument. The research is not complete until the project is complete.

Understanding and Evaluating Sources

When conducting research, students must understand the significance of the types of sources they use as evidence. Certain sources are more valued than others and offer a higher degree of support to claims. Most sources are categorized as either primary or secondary. Both primary and secondary sources are further categorized into an unofficial hierarchy of best or most valued sources. This determination is based upon several qualifying factors such as originality, credibility; wealth of scope of research involved, ethos of the author, etc. Therefore, it is imperative that students choose a variety of highly credible sources to produce their own work of research and writing. The following definitions and examples below provide a framework for understanding sources acceptable in academic research and writing. Both print and electronic sources can be of three types: primary, secondary, and tertiary. To strengthen the research component of your project, use at least some primary sources in your writing, if they are available. For example, if you are writing a critique of the president's State of the Union speech, find a copy of the original speech, perhaps at the White House site, http;//www.whitehouse.gov, or at the online New York Times, http://www.nytimes.com, which often offers full text of speeches. Then locate commentaries on his speeches, which would be secondary sources.

Primary Sources

Primary sources are those records generated by a particular event or time period, by those who participated in or witnessed it such as a records containing information documented at or about the time of the event, as opposed to compiled or secondary information; primary sources are generally more reliable than secondary sources. Primary sources contain original information and are usually the place where the original information first appears. A primary source is a person, place, or thing that provides firsthand information about something. Primary sources can be defined in two ways. (1) A document or other sort of evidence written or created during the time under study. Primary sources offer an inside view of a particular event. (2) In science, an original report of research that has not been condensed or interpreted. Because of the Internet, it is now easier for students to find primary sources such as speeches or research reports.

Types of Primary Sources

Examples of primary sources include autobiographies, speeches, official records, news film footage, original manuscripts, records, or documents providing original research or documentation, photographs, drawings, letters, diaries, books, minutes of meetings, films, posters, play scripts, speeches, songs, a first person account, interviews, speeches, results of experiments or original research, literary works, autobiographies, original theories, oral histories, a lab report, a painting, an original musical score or a court transcript, court reports, artifacts or physical objects, field research reports, technical reports, research journal articles, and conference proceedings.

Secondary Sources

A secondary source is any source that is not first hand. Secondary sources are those records generated by an event but written by non-participants of the event. Secondary sources are based on or derived from primary sources but have been interpreted or analyzed. Secondary sources are one step removed from the event being described but provide the background necessary to understand the primary sources. Secondary sources usually describe, summarize, analyze, evaluate, derive from, or are based on primary source material. Secondary sources are texts based on primary sources, and involve generalization, analysis, synthesis, interpretation, or evaluation. Information written by an authority who reports on an event, person, place or thing; i.e., a biography, is a secondary source; an autobiography is a primary source. A secondary source contains information that other people have gathered and interpreted, extended, analyzed, or evaluated.

Types of Secondary Sources

Examples of secondary sources are those that include magazine and journal articles, literary criticism, biographies, and encyclopedia articles which analyze or interpret primary sources. Others are textbooks, journal articles, histories, criticisms, commentaries, encyclopedias, and other materials that are not original manuscripts. Sometimes you can locate original sources by examining the works cited of a secondary source.

Tertiary Sources

A tertiary source is a selection and compilation of primary and secondary sources.

Types of Tertiary Sources

Examples of tertiary sources include almanacs, dictionaries, encyclopedias, and fact books, reference material that synthesizes work already reported in primary or secondary sources.

Government Documents

More and more government institutions and agencies now publish many of their documents on the World Wide Web. It certainly saves taxpayer dollars to do so, and it also makes documents more accessible to the general public. Try one or more of the gateway sites mentioned below.

FirstGov
http://www.firstgov.gov

The federal government provides FirstGov as an easy access point or "front door" which links to more 186 million Web pages from federal and state governments, most of which are not available through commercial Web sites. You can find, for example, everything from books in the Library of Congress to real-time tracking of a NASA space mission. FirstGov even offers a special Web page that collects information for students about financial aid and careers.

Thomas Legislative Information
http://thomas.loc.gov

This link provides information about pending legislation and other matters relevant to the United States Congress. It offers a full text of the Congressional Record, public laws since 1973, committee reports, and much more.

FirstGov is the federal government's gateway to Web-based information from federal and state agencies and institutions.

Federal Information Center
http://fic.info.gov

The Federal Citizen Information Center (FCIC) supplies answers to questions about consumer problems and government services. For example, if you want to know more about social security benefits, you can find a jargon-free explanation at this site. Also, it offers "before you buy" information about consumer products, as well as a list of the best places to send a consumer complaint.

The Federal Web Locator
http://www.lib.auburn.edu/madd/docs/fedloc.html

The Center for Information Law and Policy offers this gateway to federal agencies and institutions, in addition to non-government federally-related sites.

Core Documents of the U.S. Democracy
http://www.gpoaccess.gov/coredocs.html

The Government Printing Office (GPO) maintains a digital collection of the basic federal government documents that "define our democratic society." The collection includes the Constitution, the Bill of Rights, landmark Supreme Court decisions, the Budget, the Census Catalog, and the US Government Manual.

How to Evaluate Web Sources

Who Is the Author?

An important first step in establishing credibility of a Web site is considering the authorship. Credible authors that publish on the Internet generally will give a brief statement of their qualifications, or they may post a resume. If your article was published in a magazine or newspaper, search the publication for other articles by the same author. If the author has an affiliation with a university, you can search the university's Web site for additional information about the author. You can also do a keyword search for that person through a search engine.

Who Is the Publisher?

The publisher often is as important as the author. If the text was published in a reputable journal, magazine, or newspaper, the credibility of the publication attaches to the article. If your text was published on a Web site, not a publication's Web site, you need to employ other methods to assess the credibility of the publisher.

If you found the Web site through one of the librarian-research engines (pages 33-36), for example, you know the site has been evaluated and found acceptable for academic use.

You may be able to tell if the Web site is linked to an organization by looking at the URL or Web address. The organization or company name in the URL, such as http://www.exxon.com indicates that the material is published on the Exxon Web site. The suffix of the URL is also helpful: .edu means an educational or research institution, .gov for government resources, .com or .net for commercial products or commercially-sponsored sites.

Does the Document Appear Professional?

Credible sources go through an editing and reviewing process. Does the text look balanced and fair? Watch for grammatical errors, punctuation errors, misspellings, and other errors that would have been caught during an editing process. Ask yourself whether the graphics of the site add to or detract from the authoritativeness of the site.

Does It Provide Information about Sources?

Look for a list of references at the end of the document and/or informal references— to sources in the text. Where did the author get his or her information? If you cannot tell where the information came from, why should you trust it? It is a good idea to choose a few of the references the author mentions and validate them by making sure that the books or journal articles used actually exist and are represented fairly.

Is It Current?

Look for a publication date or a "last updated" date. Most credible sources will have a date. Currency can also be checked by testing out the links on the page. Are the links still up-to-date and useable? Do the graphics or photos display?

What Is the Purpose?

Was the Web site created to offer trustworthy information, to persuade, to sell, or for some other reason? If the site is selling anything, use its content only with great caution.

Evaluate Web Sources

Many people tend to believe what they see in print. They may think that if information is in a book or a news magazine, it must be true. If you read critically, however, you know that all sources must be evaluated. Does a source give a balanced reporting of the evidence, or does it display bias? What resource sources are cited? What authorities are utilized? With the Internet, perhaps even more than with print texts, it is important to evaluate your sources. Undoubtedly, much reliable and valuable information is published through the Web, and you should not hesitate to use sources that, in your judgment, are credible. Remember, though, not all information on the Web is accurate. Anyone with a Web connection and a little knowledge can create a site, and automated search engines will include that site in their databases. Also, many sites are commercial and may have their own marketing reasons for promoting certain information. Before relying on information, ask yourself the following questions listed in "How to Evaluate Web Sources."

You may intentionally study biased sources on the Web if the material are primary texts such as home pages of political candidates, special interest groups, or companies selling products. If so, do not take their information at face value. Indeed, you can make your evaluation of biased texts part of your argument. You could, for example, compare what a company selling a health food supplement such as ginkgo biloba or omega 3 oils says about that product with what you read in your search of other texts related to that product (including scientific studies). One of the Web's revolutionary aspects is that individuals and organizations can put their side of the story directly before the public. It is part of your job as a Web consumer to evaluate critically the motivation or validity of these direct-to-the-public texts.

SECTION 2

Library Tools

❋

Today's college libraries are still the best sources for current information published in books and periodicals. In addition to the familiar hard-cover books and print periodicals, libraries are increasingly offering digital resources. As a college student, you have entry through your library Web site to online books and periodical databases which have restricted access, resources you can not find directly on the Internet without paying fees.

Library Computerized Catalogs

A library computerized catalog provides bibliographical information about the library's collection. Likely, you can find call numbers and other essential location information about thousands of books, photos, videos, journals, and other items. Generally, catalogs can be accessed by keyword, subject, author, title, and call number. You may also find books which are available in digital form through the card catalog.

On the library home page, you will find links to other information and services such as database searches, interlibrary loan, and course reserves.

Types of Searches

- Keyword—Unless you know the author or title of a book, keyword is the best type of search because it finds the search word or words anywhere in the bibliographical citation.

  Example: water quality

- Title—Type the exact order of words in the title.

  Example: History of the United Kingdom

- Author—Type the author's name, putting the last name first. You don't need to include a comma.

  Example: Miller Henry J.

- Subject—Type the exact Library of Congress subject heading.

  Example: Spanish language – Grammar, Historical

- Call Number—Type the exact call number.

  Example: B851 .P49 2004

This university library Web site affords quick access to the computerized catalog, allowing searches by keywords, subject, author, title, and call number.

Library Databases

College and university libraries increasingly rely on databases to provide digital versions of articles published in journals, magazines, newspapers, as well as other publications and materials. Generally, the databases are available to students and faculty through the Internet via the library home page, though a library card and a password may be required for off-campus access.

Library databases make use of online forms similar to that of a library computerized catalog. Searches are by subject, title, author, and name of publication. Advanced search features are available. Some databases provide full text of articles published in newspapers, journals, and magazines. Others give publication information only, such as title, author, publication, date of publication, and an abstract of the article. Popular databases include Lexis-Nexis Academic Universe, Academic Search Premier, and JSTOR.

Frequently Listed Databases

Academic Search Premier

This is an EBSCOhost database that contains full-text articles for almost 4000 academic, social sciences, humanities, general science, education and multi-cultural journals, many of which are peer-reviewed. It also offers abstracts of thousands more journals. This site contains full-text articles from a number of major print magazines and newspapers (full-text coverage from 1965 to present).

ArticleFirst (FirstSearch)

This is a searchable index of articles taken from the contents pages of nearly 12,500 journals in science, technology, medicine, social science, business, the humanities, and popular culture (full-text of selected articles from 1990-present).

InfoTrac Newspapers

This site provides access to full-text articles from over a hundred regional newspapers, including the *Austin American-Statesman, Dallas Morning News*, and *Houston Chronicle.*

The UL library offers access to a variety of electronic databases and other research tools, through the web links pictured above.

INGENTA

Formerly known as Uncover, this database provides citations from 1988 to the present to articles from the tables of contents of approximately 25,000 journals and magazines that cover all disciplines. If the subscription of the university allows, you can purchase full-text articles. It can also be searched directly at http://www.gateway.ingenta.com.

JSTOR: Electronic Journal Archive

This database contains full-text articles from over 300 journals for fields including anthropology, Asian studies, ecology, economics, education, finance, history, mathematics, philosophy, political science, and sociology. Search in all journals or specify particular journals.

LexisNexis Academic

This LexisNexis database contains some 5,000 journals including full-text coverage of topics such as legal, business, government, current news, and medicine.

Newspaper Source

An EBSCOHost database, Newspaper Source offers current news from around the world with updates from newspaper wire services, as well as national and international newspapers.

Project Muse

This database offers more than 200 journal titles from the fields of literature, history, the arts, cultural studies, education, political science, gender studies, economics, and others.

PsycInfo

This is an EBSCOhost bibliographic index that provides citations, abstracts, and some full text for the field of psychology taken from journal articles, book chapters, books, dissertations, and technical reports. The coverage includes the psychological aspects of related disciplines.

Readers' Guide Abstracts

This is a FirstSearch database that corresponds to the printed *Readers' Guide to Periodical Literature*. It contains selected full-text articles from magazines on a wide variety of topics including news, arts, education, business, sports, health, consumer affairs, and others.

Worldcat

This is a FirstSearch database that provides access to library catalogs from around the world. The database contains bibliographic records describing books, journals, maps, musical scores, manuscripts, etc.

Academic Search Premier, a popular full-text database provided by EBSCOhost, is one of the many electronic resources accessible through the UL library.

Government Documents

Government documents present a wealth of information for many contemporary events and issues. Your library may be a federal depository, which means that users can locate many federal documents onsite. If so, you can look up government sources in the online library catalog.

Lexis-Nexis Congressional Universe

Congressional Universe offers an index to congressional publications, including pending legislation, the Federal Register, and other documents dating back to 1970.

Lexis-Nexis Government Periodicals Universe

Periodicals Universe gives access to periodicals published by U.S. government agencies from 1987 to the present.

Index

Ann Dobie Outstanding Freshman Essay
awards, 41
Argumentation, 52-57,
   and claims, 67-71
   forms of, 71-84
Assignments (*see also* Essays)
   in ENGL 101, 43-44
   in ENGL 102, 47
   for library research, 27-28
Audience awareness, 52-53, 56-57
   and argument, 71-83
   and thesis construction, 68-70
   as goal of first-year writing, 1, 43-44

Colons, 118 (*see also* Punctuation)
Commas, 116-117 (*see also* Punctuation)
   and sentence structure, 94-101
Course prerequisites, 3-5, 9

Edith Garland Dupre Library, 18, 25-27 (*see
also* Research)
   and electronic research, 203-207
English department, 1-2
   policies and information, 12
Essays, 51-57, 61-66, 143-58
   diagnostic, 3
   grading of, 13
   parts of, 60
   student samples of, 160-67, 186-94

First-year writing, 1-2
   and prerequisite contracts, 5, 9
   and release forms, 7, 11

Genre, 55-57
Grading Rubric, 13
Grammar exercises, 87-127

Hyphens, 119-120 (*see also* Punctuation)

MLA style, 168-94 (*see also* Research)
   annotated bibliography, 175-85
   in-text citations, 168-71
   long or block quotations, 169-70
   online sources, 170, 173-74
   parenthetical citations, 168-69
   print sources, 172-73
   sample manuscript format, 186-94
   works cited entries, 171-75
Moodle, 40

Nouns, 86-87

OWLS (online writing labs), 40

Paragraphs, 128-133
   and theses, 67-70
   and voice, 111-12
   introductory, 138-40
Parallelism, 114-15
Peer review, 29 (*see also* Revision)
   and collaborative learning, 45
   examples and process of, 134-37, 141-59
   sample handouts for, 31-36
Plagiarism, 14-23, 48
   avoiding, 18
   definition of, 14
   penalties for, 16
   types of, 15-16
Pronouns, 97-98
Punctuation, 115-120
   and credibility of web sources, 201

Reading strategies, 58-66
   and critical thinking, 51-54
   and peer review, 134-37
   as goal of first-year writing, 1, 43, 47
Research, 195-207 (*see also* MLA style)
   and genre, 54-57
   and personal experience, 141-42
   and plagiarism, 18
   and thesis construction, 67
   electronic, 203-07

types of sources used in, 196-97
understanding and evaluating sources used
in, 198-202
Revision, 131-37 (*see also* Peer review)
examples and process of, 141-59

Semicolons, 118 (*see also* Punctuation)
Sentences, 84-120
and conjugation errors, 87-88
cleft, 98-99
combining strategies for, 90-92, 94-96
fragments, 99-100
kernel, 88-92, 94-96
modeling, 96-97
redundancy in, 92-94
run-ons, 100-01
transitions between, 128-30
types of, 112-14
Southwestern Review, 40
Syllogisms, 73-74

Textbooks, 1
Thesis statements, 67-83
Transitions, 128-30

Verbs, 101-09
action, 103-05
and tense, 102
"Be," 101
Linking, 101
"reporting," 105-107
transitive and intransitive, 107-09
Voice, 141-42, 148, 155-56
active and passive, 109-112

Writing Center, 38-39
and avoiding plagiarism, 16, 18

NOTES

NOTES

NOTES